Idea-rich strategies for *'serious'* leaders

LEGACY OF LEADERSHIP

Strive for
significance
– Lead with
purpose!

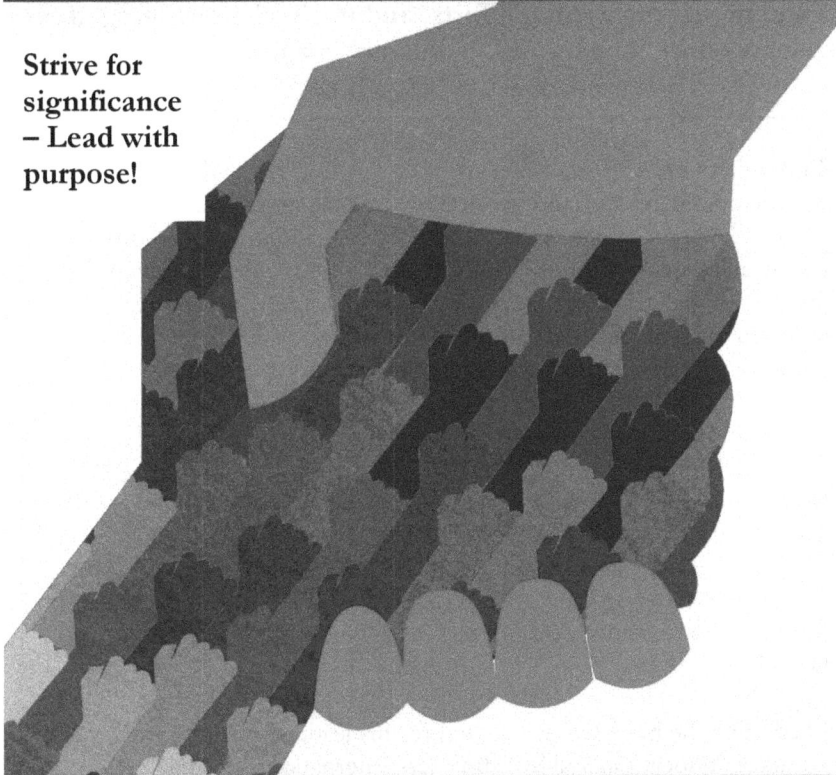

By Bob 'Idea Man' Hooey

Accredited Speaker, Spirit of CAPS recipient

6th Edition
SuccessPublications.ca

Foreword by Chris Ford, DTM, PIP,
Brigadier-General (Ret.) (Dec.)
Toastmasters International President 2007- 2008

"Legacy of Leadership – strive for significance and success, lead with purpose, and communicate with confidence. Idea-rich strategies for serious leaders. Leave behind empowered people who have the courage to step up, speak up, and successfully lead yourself and others." **Bob 'Idea Man' Hooey**

"Do not go where the path may lead, go instead where there is no path and leave a trail." **Ralph Waldo Emerson**

Dedicated to my amazing and skilled wife Irene who courageously edits and proofs my writing efforts, and to all who encouraged me in my leadership. 'Legacy of Leadership' is a team effort.

The Spirit of CAPS *may* be awarded to one CAPS member each year who demonstrates the spirit of sharing, leading, and inspiring other professional speakers, trainers, and facilitators within the mission, vision, and values of CAPS. This member will have demonstrated the qualities of generosity, spirit, and professionalism over many years and reflected outstanding credit, respect, honour, and admiration in the Association. (**Bob Hooey** was surprised with this award in November 2011 at the **Canadian Association of Professional Speakers** convention in Toronto, Ontario.)

Bob 'Idea Man' Hooey is a charter member of CAPS National (1997) and has served in a multitude of leadership roles including being Chapter President of Vancouver (1999 & 2000) as well as Edmonton (2012). He served on the CAPS National Board (2000-2002), the CAPS Editorial Board, and served (5 years) as a Trustee for the CAPS Foundation.

In addition, he has been recognized for his leadership in the National Speakers Association and Toastmasters International. He has been honoured by the United Nations Association and received the Canada 125 award for his leadership and community service. In 1998 he was inducted into Toastmasters International's Hall of Fame as the 48th speaker, world-wide, to earn their coveted professional level Accredited Speaker designation. **He continues to lead with the objective of leaving a significant positive legacy.**

Ravi Tangri, CSP, Past CAPS National President

In Memory

Christopher Kevin Ford, CD, BGen (retired), DTM
Past International President, Toastmasters International
Feb 5, 1949 – September 13, 2023

Toastmasters lost a great friend and leader recently when Chris ended his battle with ALS. His contributions to our lives and to those of us living in Canada will be long remembered and sorely missed. *I told him we were updating Legacy and would continue to use his kind foreword and he was pleased.*

This 6ᵗʰ edition is dedicated in his honor.

Chris Ford, DTM *was President (2007-08) of* **Toastmasters International – Where Leaders Are Made.** *A dedicated Toastmaster for over 4 decades, his theme for his year as president was: "Toastmasters: Shaping Ourselves… Shaping Our World!"*

Chris Ford *served in the Military Engineering branch of the Canadian Army for 35 years, retiring in 2001 as a Brigadier-General. After a few years of 'semi-self-employment' Chris returned to the Defence Department in 2006, as the Director General of Alternative Dispute Resolution. Retiring again in 2011, he was for many years a professional speaker and provided communication, leadership, and conflict management services through his consulting business called, most appropriately, "Generally Speaking". He contributed to his community at large through mentorship, public speaking and support. He saw obstacles as challenges to be tackled, with a smile on his face. He was a supportive friend to me.*

Chris Ford *was a generous contributor to our* **'In the Company of Leaders'** *anthology published in 2008, 2015, 2019 (for our 95 anniversary) which will be revised and released in 2024 in honor of Toastmasters International 100ᵗʰ anniversary. He previously contributed a chapter which will be in the 100ᵗʰ anniversary edition.*

I have been so blessed to have TM leaders like Chris Ford (dec), John Noonan (dec) Jana Barnhill, Dilip Abayasekara, Pat Johnson, and Neil Wilkinson as influencers in my life.

The names 'Toastmasters International'®, 'Toastmasters' and the Toastmasters International emblem are ® trademarks protected in the United States, Canada and other countries where Toastmasters Clubs exist. They are used in this context, anywhere mentioned, for reference in this publication. Visit www.Toastmasters.org for information on this amazing organization and the communication and leadership programs available globally.

Foreword by Chris Ford, DTM, PIP, Brigadier-General (Ret.)
International President 2007- 08 Toastmasters International

"No matter what we do, if we are always guided by our shared values of respect, integrity, service and excellence, we cannot go wrong."
Chris Ford, DTM, PIP, BRIGADIER-GENERAL (Ret.) (Dec.)

Even if I had *misspelled* that first word, it would still be right, because **this book by Bob 'Idea Man' Hooey indeed moves us forward as leaders.** Everyone wants to leave a legacy and everyone reading this book wants to become a better leader. Wanting and doing are two very different things. ***Wanting – the innate desire to acquire something or to be someone*** – is a concept we all know only too well. *"I want to have better job; I want to succeed in my graduate studies; I want to lead more effectively"*. We can **Want** all we **Want**, but **Doing** – *ah, therein lies the rub!* Transforming the want into a do-able action plan can be intimidating, challenging, postponed, or simply relegated to the *too difficult* list.

Enter the 'Idea Man'. Even though he is still very much with us (thankfully!), Bob has gifted all of us in his very readable **'Legacy of Leadership'** with a wonderfully do-able action plan. The focus and relevance of Bob's ideas are nicely summed up in his preview statements: **taking your leadership to the next level and ensuring your leadership makes a difference.** *(Bob and Chris at SOS Toastmasters)*

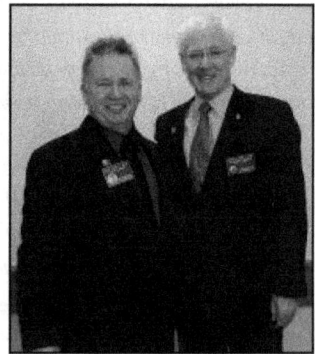

This book is not about going from zero to sixty in ten seconds, it's about incremental change; it's about striving to be just a little bit better tomorrow than today. It's about moving forward as a leader over time.

Bob challenges us to ensure our leadership makes a difference.

Our leadership must make a positive difference in the lives of the men and women whom we lead. Otherwise, we have no business calling ourselves leaders.

Read this book! But don't just read it; don't just want to become a better leader. The 'Idea Man' offers 'YOU' ideas and insights and pragmatic guidance which will lead you to your success as a leader.

Now all you have to do is just do it!

Chris Ford, DTM, PIP, Brigadier-General (Ret.) (Dec.)
International President 2007- 08 Toastmasters International

© *Chris Ford, All rights reserved. Included with kind permission of the author.*

Chris left a real legacy of leadership in our lives. RIP

We need men and women who are committed to equipping and motivating those who would follow them to grow, become more productive, and succeed. **We need YOU; as active leaders who strive for significance vs. success and who will lead on purpose.**

It is my quest to provide a few idea-rich tools, tips, and techniques which will assist you in your own leadership journey. Is this publication complete? No, but it is finished, now, for this updated 6th edition (2024).☺ As with our other publications, we'll revisit it from time to time to tweak and add new lessons learned and insights garnered from working with other leaders or in reading from experts in this field.

I invite you to keep in touch and share your own lessons and challenges in your leadership legacy. I believe we each leave a legacy behind – our choice is in leaving a positive, productive one which made a difference in the lives of our staff and our clients. That my friends, is significance.

Bob 'Idea Man' Hooey, bhooey@mcsnet.ca

Some short leadership videos throughout this 6th edition for your personal use. Simply follow the link to my YouTube channel to play them. (80 leadership ones to date and more to follow)
https://www.youtube.com/user/ideamanbob

"A Leader...

I went on a search to become a leader.

*I searched high and low. I spoke with authority. People listened.
But alas, there was one who was wiser than I, and the crowd
followed that individual.*

*I sought to inspire confidence, but the crowd responded,
"Why should we trust you?"*

*I postured, and I assumed the look of leadership with a countenance
that flowed with confidence and pride. But many passed me by and
never noticed my air of elegance.*

*I ran ahead of the others, pointed the way to new heights.
I demonstrated that I knew the route to greatness. And then
I looked back, and I was alone.*

*"What shall I do?" I queried. "I've tried hard and used all that I know."
And I sat down and pondered long.*

*And then I listened to the voices around me. And I heard what the
group was trying to accomplish. I rolled up my sleeves and joined
in the work.*

*As we worked, I asked, "Are we all together in what we want to do
and how to get the job done?"*

*I found myself encouraging the fainthearted. I sought the ideas of
those too shy to speak out. I taught those who had little skill.
I praised those who had worked hard. When our task was completed,
one of the group turned to me and said, "This would not have been
done but for your leadership."*

*At first, I said, "I didn't lead. I just worked with the rest." And then I
understood, leadership is not a goal. It's a way of reaching a goal.*

I lead best when I help others to go where we've decide to go.

I lead best when I help others to use themselves creatively.

*I lead best when I forget about myself as a leader and focus on my
    group ...their needs and their goals."*

Anonymous

I can't remember who originally shared this poem with me. I have
shared it and/or included it in numerous articles and leadership
publications. **'Legacy of Leadership'** would seem naked without it.

Table of contents

"Avoid being the blind leading the blind… leave behind a legacy of leadership!"

Bob 'Idea Man' Hooey

Thanks for investing your time in reading, reflecting, and acting on the information we've compiled and created, just for you.

Our world needs '*serious*' leaders; men and women who are willing to step up and speak up. We need more 'serious' leaders in our society and my wish is this publication will give you and your team some practical tips and guidelines in that noble quest. **Strive for significance – lead on purpose!** I wish you all the best for your leadership journey.

Bob 'Idea Man' Hooey, DTM, PDG, Past Region Advisor
Accredited Speaker, Certified Kitchen Designer-Emeritus

Bob also authored: 'Power of One!'; 'The Courage to Lead'; 'Creating Time to Sell, Lead, or Manage'; 'Speaking for Success'; and 'In the Company of Leaders' (*See page 134 for a complete list of his idea-rich publications*)

https://youtu.be/HRN0HyChtvg *Bob in Paris -European Speakers Summit*
https://youtu.be/-fAFD9mkUPo *Bob's demo video*

Each life a legacy – lead on purpose!
Idea-rich strategies for 'serious' leaders

"Our life and work are a portrait of who we are – autograph them both with style!"   *Anonymous*

The *tapestry of our lives* is inter-woven with the lives and enriched with the ideas of those we connect with daily. Whether we realize it or not, our life leaves a *legacy*. The stories of our leadership, and activities become a *living legend*.

"People will talk about you – why not give them something positive to say?" ☺ *Bob Hooey*

Our daughter Amanda pictured in front of Luzan Grocery which was once in the family and now at the Ukrainian Village east of Edmonton, AB

People we know, work, or live with, have a lasting impression based on their personal experience with us. Why is it then that we wait until they are gone or have moved on to acknowledge the important people in our life? **Life is a *continuous* choice**… choose wisely!

I have lived in the country north-east of Edmonton, Alberta for 23 years now. It is a quiet, rustic, creative type of life; a place for me to write and prepare as I still travel to present around the world. Driving the *rural* roads, I see dilapidated, boarded-up buildings, vacant stores, gas stations, and shops that once housed thriving businesses, stores, entrepreneurial dreams that profitably served their communities and customers. **I wonder, what happened?**

- Did the business thrive and move to a better location? Did they neglect their clients? Did the market leave them behind?

- Did it miss the changes in client needs and slowly die?
- Did their competition do a better job?
- Did they fall behind in technology? Service? Products?
- Did their clients desert them? What makes the difference?

I also see thriving, prosperous businesses, too, in attractive, spruced-up, well-lit buildings; well-stocked and open for business to profitably serve both their clients and their communities.

I also see homes previously inhabited by families with dreams of building a life together. Houses left to fall apart, torn and worn by the winds and the rain. Houses left to the elements when the people who lived there moved on. I wonder, what happened? Yet, I also see some older homes, lovingly cared for, passed on from family-to-family, still vibrant with life. In fact, mine, built in 1955, fits that description. ☺ What made the difference, I wonder?

What legacy is being told of you and your team every day?

When you're done working, what leadership legacy would you like to leave behind? What are they saying about you right now? What picture would you like your team, your clients, and the community to see and remember about your contributions and work?

What would be the ultimate comment or testimonial on your life and contributions in pioneering and living life as an adventure?

Why not leave a *lasting legacy;* a history of strong dynamic leadership that has contributed in a positive way? A legacy of leadership that has engaged, inspired, challenged, and cared for the many you led.

Once we understand that we do leave a *legacy of leadership* behind, we can make a conscious choice to ensure it is a positive one. We can *choose* to invest our time, resources, and energies in those activities and organizations that create lasting value; as well as in the lives of those we love and respect.

As 'serious' leaders we have that opportunity to invest in the lives and success of those we lead. This investment can leave a lasting *legacy* in their lives and the lives of those they touch.

My parents both passed away in 1999, leaving a big hole in the lives of my sister and myself. More importantly, Mom and Dad left a *legacy of love and commitment to community service that* has been ingrained in our lives. Their *legacy* lives on in our lives and in the conversations I now share.

Acknowledge the accomplishments and contributions of those around you!

I've learned people too often die *under-acknowledged*, under-valued, and under-appreciated. This is one of the biggest losses in our rich culture and legacy as a culture. This is the biggest loss in the changing tapestry of any living organization or group. We have people who have made a *genuine* difference and *lasting* impact in our lives. However, ***they don't know – because we never told them!***

Resolve to tell these men and women now!

Tell them often how *important* they are in your life NOW and *where* they have made a difference! Share their legacy and their story. This can be the most valuable gift you can give them. This can be such a wonderful legacy as a leader – to tell your people **now** how and why you appreciate them and to share positive encouragement as they seek to grow in their respective roles.

Investing in the lives of others can be our best legacy! Let them tell your story!

I've often heard, *"You can't take it with you!"* Interesting thought! This is true. When we pass away, we leave behind everything we *'once held'* important. I've yet to see a hearse pulling a U-Haul trailer.☺ When we take personal leadership with our time, skills, and resources, we can then *invest* them in the lives of people we want to help now.

Think of each person who has invested in your life and your success to date. Some have passed away and some have moved on to different roles and careers. Their investment in you is *still* paying dividends, *still* adding to their legacy as you continue to grow and pass on what they taught you.

You have been given an opportunity to *pass it forward* to your team and clients. Share their legacy or idea-rich stories with your employees as examples of what they can aspire to become. Your most important activity and use of time is investing in your team for their success. Your gift, your real legacy as a leader, is based on equipping them to win. **You win when they win!**

Realize the impact you have and choose to make it a positive and dynamic one!

As leaders, we influence and make an impact on the lives of others each day and in each encounter, we have with them. This too is part of our lasting legacy as caring and courageous leaders.

We have an impact on people whom we may not even know. *The legacy continues*... as people tell *our* stories. Like the ripples on a lake that bounce off each other, we do have an impact and we change the patterns of those we connect with, as do those who connect us.

One of the most decisive decisions I ever made was striving to ensure **my life makes a difference,** to leave behind a *positive* legacy of leadership. To ensure the men and women in my life knew how much I *truly* appreciated them. To leave a *legacy of empowered* and encouraged people, audiences, readers, family, and friends who know I loved and cared enough to give my very best. Who know I believed in them and prayed for their success in life! Ensuring my words, both written and verbal, were based in truth, delivered in love, focused on enhancing the positive opportunities in life. I have stumbled at times, but I got up and continued to serve and lead. You can too!

The world needs courageous men and women who are willing to step up and take their leadership role seriously in tackling these pressures and challenges.

Whether your leadership path is personal, as a volunteer, serving as an elected official, or is organizational (positional) you do and will make a difference. Choose to make it a positive one!

Taking personal responsibility for your own growth and success in that leadership role is worth the investment. This is where you apply '*leverage*' to dynamically succeed!

Personal leadership – 'The Power of One!' leads to engaging the passion of many and allows you to walk 'In The Company of Leaders'. *(Both books are available from www.SuccessPublications.ca)*

Thank you for investing your time in reading and allowing me to be a part of your on-going legacy. **I wish you significance in your quest to be a more influential, serious, and effective leader.**

"If you would not be forgotten, as soon as you are dead and rotten, either write things worth reading, or do things worth the writing."

Benjamin Franklin

What is your leadership style? Perhaps a blend works best!

- **Pacesetter:** "Do as I do, now!"
- **Authoritative:** "Come with me!"
- **Affiliative:** "People come first!"
- **Coach:** "Try this!"
- **Coercive:** "Do what I tell you!"
- **Democratic:** "What do you think?"

From Daniel Goleman's *Leadership That Gets Results* and his study of 3000 middle-level managers. He found that style can be responsible for up to 30% of company's bottom line profitability. Creating a blend of leadership styles can elevate and inspire your team.

Getting started

Welcome fellow leaders! Welcome to the *never-ending* journey of an evolving career and management focus on personal leadership development and coaching. Whether your leadership is career or community based we can help. Change in global perspective has placed a new focus and pressure on finding and applying more productive uses of your assets and updating your team members' skills to compete successfully.

Taking personal leadership in your own career growth and success is worth the investment. This is where you apply *leverage* to dynamically succeed! Too many leaders are seemingly *blind* to the opportunities and responsibilities of creating and nurturing those who would follow them. Too many miss the opportunity (are blind) to play an active part in the selection, growth, and success of those who would succeed them; those who would help them succeed as leaders.

> *"Avoid being the blind leading the blind ... leave behind a 'Legacy of Leadership'."* **Bob 'Idea Man' Hooey**

One quick comment on leadership. Leaders come in all shapes, sizes, and roles within society. Some might be military or political leaders, like **Ukrainian President Volodymyr Zelensky** who is actively leading his countrymen in resistance to Russian invaders sent by a petty tyrant, named Putin. Some are actively involved in business, community, or association leadership, like my good Toastmasters' friend **Peter Kossowan** who has started more clubs than anyone in our 100-year history. Each has a different focus and path; and each has lessons to teach us as we forge ahead and create our leadership legacy.

The lessons included in **Legacy of Leadership** can be applied wherever your leadership path may lead.

Leadership can be a *lonely* and *frustrating* road to walk. There will be times when you wonder if it is *worth the effort* you give. I know I have! **'Legacy of Leadership - Idea-rich strategies for serious leaders'** is my contribution to helping you work through the frustrations, challenges, and lessons; to see your efforts bear positive fruit. Being a leader is a lifetime commitment and we need you.

This book was updated (2024) to share tips and idea-rich techniques we felt would be helpful in your quest for significance.

In more recent history, workplace coaching has taken on a new, effective focus. Leading edge employees, managers, and successful executives have experienced positive results from enlisting the help of a leadership coach to help them improve in specific areas or to achieve specific goals. **Striving for significance leads along this path.**

People have been going outside the corporate arena and enlisting or recruiting personal or leadership coaches. They want to change, to improve their performance, and to enhance their ability to win! Strive for significance - lead on purpose!

Many world leaders, executives, and innovative managers have also seen the wisdom and a positive return on their investment of time and resources in training and **coaching their employees and future leaders for optimal results**.

Things are changing in the boardrooms, factories, and on the sales floors of businesses across North America and the globe. **Are you?** Leaders are changing as well, with more women taking on important leadership roles and proving themselves worthy as they inspire other women to follow their lead. Bravo!

People generally experience problems and challenges in their performance for four major reasons:
- Poor or inadequate training
- Inadequate equipment or support services
- Time constraints and poor time management
- Motivation

Unfortunately, many of these reasons can be traced back to poor or *uninspired* leadership.

Many 21st Century leaders are moving into the coaching role as an effective style and skill in helping their teams grow and succeed.

- **Leadership coaching** in its essence will help you discover the area(s) which are acting as roadblocks for the person being coached.
- **Leadership coaching** can help you turn roadblocks into stepping-stones for increased success, productivity, and a real sense of satisfaction on the job.
- **Leadership coaching** can bring you a sense of satisfaction as the coach, too — **bringing out the best and in seeing your people productively grow and win!**

One of the most important aspects of your leadership growth and continued success is measured by the investment in your team and the results of those efforts.

"You win, when your people win!" **Bob 'Idea Man' Hooey**

I had the opportunity to repeatedly drive this idea-rich strategy home a few years back when I was engaged to work with the President and senior management team for one of **Canada's 50 Best Managed Companies.**

Over a period of four months, we explored ways of helping these men and women hone their leadership skills to better lead their respective teams. The results were astounding! The following year they broke the billion-dollar retail sales mark for the first time in their 33-year history.

This is a lesson learned from working with and studying the actions of North America's leaders in various industries, including the volunteer sector.

This, coupled with my own experience in a variety of leadership roles, has reinforced my contention that **"You win, when your team wins!"**

'Legacy of Leadership' was originally published as an e-book in 2006. We updated it in 2013, 2016, 2019, 2022 and now again in 2024 in print and e-pub as I've learned a few more lessons and tips in my own leadership journey. ☺

I trust you will find solid value in what is shared here and use it to create a **significant legacy of leadership**.

Bob 'Idea Man' Hooey
A *'serious'* leader in progress

"Leadership is both and art and a skill. Each can be enhanced by focused discipline and applied study. They continue to be honed and polished as we grow."

Bob 'Idea Man' Hooey

I'm often asked, *"Can you share an example of effective leadership?"*

Perhaps the ability to make sound decisions quickly and act on them would be one.

Providing timely and constructive feedback as well as clear instructions and expectations would be a second.

Creating a working environment that encourages employees to freely share opinions, concerns, ideas, or differing viewpoints would be a 3rd.

An environment that challenges them to challenge themselves and think creatively.

Can you think of examples in your own experience?

How to get the best use from
Your 'Legacy of Leadership'

'Legacy of Leadership' contains a range of tips, techniques, and idea-rich strategies which can help you improve the way you recruit, train, and lead your team for shared growth and long-term success. **It was <u>not</u> originally envisioned as a book**, but as a course guide for programs delivered then, by the author, in various Vancouver, British Columbia colleges and organizations. It evolved into its present form with the inclusion of stories, ideas, and first-hand experiences based on copious conversations and observations of fellow leaders. It was made *personal* from my own experiences in leading and being on a variety of leadership teams across North America and the globe.

This is not <u>just</u> a book for casual reading. It is a book to be **used**, to be dipped into, and **leveraged** as a resource or reference guide. It is your resource, so mark it, highlight it, and make notes in the margins.

To get the best from this book, first visit the **Table of Contents** to identify which chapters and/or relevant topics meet your most critical, time sensitive needs. Read them carefully and make sure you understand the guidelines and advice given. Some of the topics may not be of direct interest to you (now) depending on your needs. You may wish to read some of the other chapters so that you can understand the needs of other leaders or leadership scenarios.

'Legacy of Leadership' does not contain ALL the answers. It is a collection of thoughts, notes, clippings, tips, techniques, lessons learned, and ideas shared primarily from *one leader's viewpoint*, mine. It is simply intended as an aid to your reflection, learning, and inspiration – a resource that you can draw upon in preparation for your leadership endeavors. Its aim is to give you a creative resource that, when applied and practiced with real teams, will help you develop and build both your confidence and competence as a leader.

A more *productive approach* would be to take the tips and concepts presented here and blend them with your own leadership style, personality, and creativity. Keep in mind your own time constraints and **'comfort zone as a leader'**, to generate unique and personalized ideas on how you can create, give, and improve your interaction and action with your teams.

This book is designed to offer you flexibility in how you use it.

1) You can sit down for an hour or two and read it **cover to cover**. This is a great way to start by getting a feel for what is included, especially for newer or emerging leaders who want to gain the full benefit from their investment.

A word of advice: 'Legacy of Leadership' *is the result of over 29 plus years of personal study and first-hand experience in a variety of leadership, coaching, and support roles for executive clients. It might seem overwhelming or a bit confusing at first with the range of information included here. Once you have done a quick read the whole book, then identify sections or tips that interest you and work on more manageable chunks at a time.*

2) You can select one **chapter** or **section** at a time and work to incorporate the ideas you discover into your own leadership style and specific leadership role or situation.
3) You can look at the **Table of Contents** and jump straight to the tips or areas of study that particularly interest you.

We have attempted to incorporate something of benefit for everyone, regardless of your current level or skill in leadership. You might even find some contradictory advice in different parts of the book! This is because there is no single, universal **"right answer"** – you must find what is right for you, your objective, and your team's specific needs. What works for you is what is best. Choose it, try it, and adapt it as needed to serve you in your quest to be a more powerful and impactful leader.

"Leaders (real leaders) gain their greatest satisfaction from seeing their team grow and win in their changing roles."
Bob 'Idea Man' Hooey

Leadership, creativity, and strategic thinking

"Leadership is lifting a person's vision to higher sights, raising a person's performance to a higher standard, and building a personality beyond its normal limitations."

Peter Drucker

The foundation of **effective, creative** leadership success starts with each person taking **personal** responsibility and leadership for their own actions as part of a group; in feeling confident enough to suggest and accept revisions in team goals and performance.

You might be asking:
- *"What does 'MY' leadership have to do with vision or creativity?"*
- *"What does vision or creativity have to do with strategic leadership?"*

Quite frankly, everything! The focus of **'Legacy of Leadership'** is about *strategically* honing your skills as a creative leader and teaching those skills to your team so they succeed! **You win when they win!**

Is your goal to successfully learn *new styles* of applied problem-solving and innovation, unlock your creativity, and increase your ability to make decisions? I trust so! You must be willing to take personal leadership using new skills in your activities and in the interaction with your fellow workers, teams, suppliers, and clients. Remember, **consistent use and improvement help sharpen your skills.**

Peter Drucker wisely wrote, *"Management is doing things right; Leadership is doing the right things."*

Our goal in effectively handling opportunities for growth, problems, challenges, and mistakes is in being able to cut through to the *root* causes, in *mining* deep, and in developing real solutions to put into action in conjunction with your various teams.

It is also in providing solid *visionary* leadership that inspires those who follow you. **My objective** is to assist you to review and acquire new creative leadership skills and problem-solving models. In addition, introduce some new creativity tools to help you in your personal life, leadership, career, and interaction with your clients, staff, and co-workers. **My objective** is to help you and your team discover new approaches to the problems you may encounter in the normal course of business growth and management. **Your challenge** is to see them as opportunities to grow and change the way you live, lead, and conduct your business.

- **What is it about leaders that make them seem to stand out from the crowd?**
- **What is it about leaders that capture the hearts and minds of those who follow their direction and guidance?**

A wise man told me that... *"My ability to earn would be directly dependent on my ability to solve problems and to help people make decisions."* That sounds like effective leadership and a dash of salesmanship mixed in for good measure.

In business, we are paid for our ability to creatively solve our client's problems, through the provision of *profitable* services or products. Our stock in trade as an executive, salesperson, or leader, creativity is how we serve and solve our client and staff needs. **Each of the tools and tips shared can be applied in at least three leadership directions.**

- Problem-solving and decision making on all levels.
- Strategic planning and training your staff to grow and win.
- Tapping your inner genius to make innovation a solid part of your leadership and business focus.

"Our productivity - often our survival - does not depend solely on how much effort we expend; but on whether or not the effort we invest is in the right direction."

Bob 'Idea Man' Hooey

Experience teaches the tips, tools, and techniques we cover here **will help you in:**

- The process of defining your vision or direction.
- Outlining the processes, you need to successfully reach the goals you visualize and set for yourself and/or your team.
- Birthing and nurturing your dreams for new products, innovative processes, and profitable services.
- Solving perplexing problems for your team members and clients you encounter enroute.

Here are some objectives and benefits of ***unleashing*** your creative and constructive leadership:

- **More accurate information** – increased productivity facilitated by better communication. *(see Speaking for Success)*
- **Effective coordination** of activities – *"How do I fit in the big picture?"* – decreased duplication and wasted resources.
- **Improving the flow of ideas** - both internally (up and down) and externally – generating better buy-in and team energies.
- **Facilitating the decision-making process** – being an agent of change not just being on the receiving end of change.
- **Training** – cross training, uniform training, and an interactive forum for an honest exchange of ideas and feedback.
- **Building morale** – encouraging teamwork and mutual support which has a direct impact on morale within an organization.

Accomplishment of any or all these objectives will assist you to be a more effective leader and creatively help you prepare your team to win. We need to pause, to gain a higher perspective, to make sure we are still leading in the right direction. Then boldly move forward.

If we are not going where we want in pursuit of our focus and goals, our efficiency and effectiveness will be misdirected and disappointing.

Pause, refocus, and redirect!

Waves crashing on the shore south of Cape Town, Southern Africa remind us that there is an ebb and flow to life and leadership.

Sometimes you must let your outdated expectations go.

A few years back, I served as *reluctant* President for a struggling professional speakers' group in BC. At the end of my term, I lamented our seeming 'lack' achievement.

One of my board members reminded me that we had: stopped the bleeding (cash flow), changed our monthly educational programs to be richer and more flexible, and our CAPS National body recognized us as the chapter with the highest percentage of membership retention. **We don't always see our accomplishments the way others do.**

Two idea-rich leadership lessons

One of the biggest lessons about leadership and creative problem solving: **there is ALWAYS a solution.** Frequently, there are a **multitude of solutions.**

Leadership development, with its respective challenges, is no different. There are a multitude of opportunities to support and reinforce your abilities and skills leading and helping your team navigate the challenges you share. This is where you bring your creativity to bear.

If your leadership problem is *industry specific* you might want to talk to others in your industry and **"Thunder-think"** (*Bob's version of brainstorming*) some answers or bring it to your next Chamber of Commerce, trade, or professional association meeting.

The second lesson: **You are not the ONLY one with a problem.**

While I served on the National Speakers Association's **Chapter Leadership Council,** *we shared challenges our respective Chapters were encountering. Someone usually had a suggestion that would help which we could pass along.*

Sharing a problem can help in finding the *key* to solving it. Someone not directly involved in your problem may see a solution or thread that unravels it, due to the difference in his or her perspective or experience. Because they are not *emotionally* involved, they can see it with objectivity and perhaps more clarity! Be open to ask for help!

I believe passionately in the information I present and enjoy the opportunity to pass on my lessons; learned, at times, from magnificent failures. I'd love to share and see my **Ideas At Work!** directly or indirectly with you and your team members. I trust you will find it valuable. Our primary purpose is to see you succeed and do whatever possible to facilitate that leadership process.

At **Ideas At Work!** — we want to see you use this information in your dealings with each other and serving the needs your teams and clients. Call us to explore how we can help you and your teams.

> *"The challenge of leadership is to be strong, but not rude; be kind, but not weak; be bold, but not bully; be thoughtful, but not lazy; be humble, but not timid; be proud, but not arrogant; have humour, but without folly."*
>
> **Jim Rohn**

How to Handle the Idea Killers in Your Life!

YOU have this great dream or this fantastic idea bursts into your head. You're excited about the unlimited possibilities and can't wait to share it with your staff, co-workers, closest friends, and, of course, family.

What is their reaction? All too often, their initial reaction is to ridicule the idea, to point out its flaws, to remind you about your lack of education, your lack of money, your lack of experience, or to point out how so and so tried it and it didn't work. Whew! The result ... too often, you stop and let your dreams die, be minimized, or give up on your ideas. You've let your staff, colleagues, friends, and family opinions and criticism rob you of your future and your solid potential for greatness!

Why do they do that? Well, it might be for a variety of reasons, some of them with the best intentions. It might simply be their concern to see you avoid getting hurt or to sidestep what they see as a path to failure.

It may be, and often is, based on their 'own fears' projected onto your actions and life. It might be due to a personal failure on their part and a fear that, if you succeed, they will lose you. Or a fear they will have to deal with the reality that, just maybe, they could have done something about their 'seemingly impossible' situation. Your *potential for success* scares them or makes them a bit nervous about their own chances, neglect, or inactivity.

As leaders, how do we handle these 'helpers' or **'idea killers'** in our life or organizations? One of the best ways is to be aware of their existence and seek to avoid them in areas of vulnerability. I don't mean to cut them off completely.

Just realize that they are not committed to or understanding of your dreams and desires. Be kind, as they do not know that they don't get it. Don't waste your energy on them.

Make a conscious choice to keep these areas private, especially during the embryonic or incubation stages of establishing your goals, dreams, or ideas. Maintain your focus and keep moving forward to see your idea or dream become a reality.

As someone once wrote, **"Show no regrets for the past, no fear for the future. Expect to win – expect GREATNESS!"**

As a leader, if you refuse to accept anything but the best, you often get it! We may not get to choose our family, but we do have full control over our friends and over the amount of time we spend with colleagues, friends, and family. This is where we make the decisions and connections that help shape or determine our destiny.

In life and business, there are those who would kill our dreams and those who would, if asked, help nurture our dreams. We can identify and choose each group in which to associate and productively invest our time. Find and support your champions!

As a leader, one of the most effective ways of dealing with an idea killer is by **doing your homework**. If you have researched your dream and have done your due diligence, some can even be brought around to being 'at least' a neutral observer. When you succeed, watch them come out!

Use feedback from these idea killers as mirrors that may show you your 'blind spots'. Often, they see things that you might miss in the heat of passion. Keep in mind their input is for **information 'only'** and check it for relevance and accuracy before you allow it to impact or influence your decisions.

Demonstrate by your strategic actions that you're committed to seeing 'this' project through to completion. Often, our past track record of starting and not completing projects may influence their support and enthusiasm. This is especially true with immediate family members.

Idea killers may occasionally become allies, but it takes massive work on your part to win them over to your team.

Keep focused on your Goals and Dreams!

Don't let another person's critical attitude determine your worth or your future. Don't let them stop you! You don't know how high you can fly until you spread your wings and take to the sky. Please don't let another person's limiting beliefs, no matter how well-intentioned, stop you attempting to dream big, to compete for the ultimate prize, achieving your personal or professional dream. Create the future you imagine! **You can do it!**

It is too easy for those around you, who are hopelessly mired in their own mediocrity, to criticize you for trying to follow your dream or acting to implement your great idea.

"A rock pile ceases to be a rock pile the moment a single man contemplates it, bearing within him the image of a cathedral."
Antoine de Saint-Exupery – The Little Prince

Teamwork doesn't always work! – Here's why

Teamwork FAILS because many organizations use committees, not teams, and don't realize the difference. Lead on purpose – strive for significance vs. simply seeking success. Look to create team *effectiveness* instead!

What can you do, as the leader, to help your teams grow together and hone their individual skills?

Each team member has different drives, dreams, and challenges. Your role is to help them win! That is the true essence and power of 'serious' leadership. You can choose to make a strategic difference in people's lives.

Leadership observations

"Learning is the essential fuel for leaders, the source of high-octane energy that keeps up the momentum by continually sparking new understanding, new ideas, and new challenges. It is absolutely indispensable under today's conditions of rapid change and complexity. Very simply, those who do not learn do not long survive as leaders."

Warren Bevis & Burt Nanus

Here are some leadership ideas drawn from observations and lessons learned first-hand from a wide range of leaders. I have been blessed with some great role models – leaders in business, industry, professional and association management, community service, Toastmasters; my NSA, GSF, and CAPS colleagues; and from my parents, my wife, and my close friends. Here are shared characteristics observed from the leaders in my life and experience.

Leaders are not born

Leaders emerge and need to be nurtured by other leaders who see their potential. Leadership is a learned skill, honed by experience, and by finding the inner motivational points that inspire people to assume leadership in various aspects of their lives. Leaders are *revealed* when people see value and follow their direction. *I often saw this first-hand in my Toastmasters and CAPS leadership. When I approached people and asked them to tackle a challenge, they often took personal leadership and championed its eventual success.*

Leaders are open to change

Leaders have the courage to lead change **and** to deal with change. Positive change often happens when someone takes personal leadership and responsibility in a situation and is open to grow.

Leaders develop a sense of adventure and a realization that change is not always a *negative* event. Leaders see themselves as **catalysts** for innovative change. A true leader will see the plateau or status quo as an opportunity or foundation to move ahead and make positive changes.

Leaders are creative

Leaders are flexible to find solutions to common challenges. Often it is the creative approach that shows the way out of the problem or mess at hand. This creative outlook may even create new products or entire industries. The leader looks for that creative or innovative *twist* which will unlock the secret to solving the challenge. They are persistent in looking for innovative ways to solve problems and will inspire others to do the same.

Leaders make mistakes and build on lessons learned

Life is about learning and leadership even more so. Leaders take *calculated* risks and sometimes they make mistakes or fail. The difference, *true* leaders understand this and learn from the experience. This is a great part of the leadership process! Failure fuels their determination to succeed. They will move ahead, better informed, striving for the next opportunity to **'lead and learn'**.

Leaders are forged in the heat of reality, moulded on the anvil of adversity, and formed by the hammers of life

Personal leadership emerges in the heat of the worst challenges and conditions in your life. You can choose to take personal responsibility for your leadership role and abilities to act. I have seen the most unlikely men and women take this leadership role when the going was tough or the odds overwhelming – and succeed where others simply complained or quit trying. **Leaders don't quit; they quietly find the strength and keep going.**

Leaders are more often readers

This may not hold true of every leader. However, many of those men and women I have grown to respect make *selective* reading a definite part of their leadership growth path. They read outside their own areas of knowledge, experience, and industries. They are open to learn from a myriad of sources. They have found that in a multitude of counsel there is wisdom. *Fortunately for me, they were open to share it.*

Reading allows you to access the wisdom of the ages from leaders long gone as well as from current and emerging thought leaders. Selective, strategic reading provides value-added information that allows you to explore new ideas, new methods, and new ways of thinking. It gives you the leadership and career development ammunition you need to set, stretch, and successfully reach your goals.

Visit: **www.SuccessPublications.ca** for information on Bob's leadership, career, and business success publications.

Leaders are the foundation upon which our long-term success is given substance

In my life this is certainly true! I can look back to the pivotal points in my life and often there was the guiding, supportive hand of a leader who invested in my life, growth, and well-being.

You might see parallels in your own life and career. So many men and women and organizations have played a role in helping me hone my talents and enhance my skills which allowed me to discover that I had hidden leadership strengths and skills. Too many to thank here.

I have been humbled by their investment, encouragement, and the recognition I have garnered along the way.

"My continued leadership growth and sharing of my leadership lessons are my gift back to them for the faith they showed in my life. Leadership is a 'giving back' lifestyle of choice and commitment."
Bob 'Idea Man' Hooey

A leadership review or check-up

Reflect on these probing questions around your leadership role, responsibility, and skill. Briefly record your thoughts. Being honest in recognizing your strengths and focused areas of growth is one of the characteristics of the top-level leaders. Asking for help or getting coaching is another leadership success characteristic.

What is your *personal vision* for your leadership role?

What are your specific *areas* of responsibility?

What *strengths* and *skills* do you bring to the role?

What leadership areas do you need *help* in developing?

Where do you need to draw on the skills of your fellow leaders or employees?

Perhaps engage a leadership or team development coach or speaker? I do make on-site calls! ☺ www.ideaman.net

---

What are some of the better characteristics or traits of good leadership skills for us to emulate?

- **Flexible: leadership is constantly in play**
- **Proactive: thinking several steps ahead – plan ahead**
- **Respect: bedrock of team effectiveness**
- **Good communication: listen to feedback as well as sharing ideas. Confidence and a sense of humour help too.**
- **Delegation: effective leaders are supportive delegators**

Seven laws of leadership

Here is a quick synopsis of my opening keynote for 600 plus Alberta mayors, reeves, and councillors in Edmonton, Alberta. These **Seven Laws of Leadership** served as the core part of my remarks at their Annual General Meeting. **A few remarks to precede those points...**

Perhaps you've seen the movie **Lincoln**, released back in 2012. I did and it refreshed my appreciation for the amazing role he played during a dark period of challenge. This is where real leadership shines – in the darkness of a tremendous seemingly unsolvable challenge.

President Abraham Lincoln led the Northern States through one of the bloodiest and darkest pages in US history. He saw the concept of keeping both sides together as something worth fighting for... and fight he did! Sadly, he did not live to see his dream of a re-unified United States take place. His focused leadership laid the foundations for this outcome.

His *legacy of leadership* lives on in the proud nation and neighbour to our south.

A few years back, while speaking in the area, I visited Ford Theater in Washington, DC where he was shot. I sat quietly, *reverently* in the seats below *his* box to get a true sense of the place. I imagined how the evening played out. I toured the basement museum where they had gathered many items including his blood-spattered clothing. I gained a much greater respect for the challenges he faced.

As leaders we will face challenges, both external and internal. Our character and our skills will be revealed and polished as we face each one. Those we would lead will look 'to' us and 'at' us in this respect.

Here are some areas of consideration (Leadership laws) I shared for us to be effective and influential leaders:

Example – people need to be able to depend on your leadership.

Today, more than ever, people are looking for leaders who will lead by example in their dealings with people and their lifestyles.

Communication – people need to know and understand what you are saying.

Today, more than ever, people are looking for clarity and consistency in our written and oral communications. They are looking for honesty and openness in the dialogue they have with us as leaders.

Ability – you need to be capable of leading other people.

Today, more than ever, people are looking for more than a slick appearance. They want content and proven ability they can trust to get them through the increasing challenges of the 21st Century.

Motivation – you need to know why YOU want to be a leader.

Today, more than ever, people want to know *why* you are doing what you are doing and so do you! A simple *"trust me"* won't cut it. This is even more noticeable with the current crop of 16-24-year-olds who are affectionately dubbed, "Generation WHY?"

Authority – people need to respond to your leadership.

Today, more than ever, people want to be able to see demonstrated commitment and power in your decisions and authority in your actions.

Strategy – you need to know where you are going.

Today, more than ever, people want to know you have a plan; one that is well thought out, covering all the contingencies and challenges.

They frequently want to know the details of that strategy before they agree to follow you.

> **Love and compassion – you need to care for the people around you.**

Today, more than ever, people want to know and see that you truly care about them, their needs, their concerns, their fears, their dreams, and their well-being. Lip service, hype, or idle words will not cut it on the 21st Century leadership track. You need to actively lead!

Take a serious look at your current leadership skill levels in light of these seven laws.

"I hear and I forget.

I see and I remember.

I do and I understand!"

Confucius

Those you would hope to lead will be and they are constantly judging your actions, attitudes, and motivation.

- What do you see?
- Are there areas where improvement is needed?
- Do you need help to overcome challenges?
- When will you start and what will you do?

I've included leadership videos as a bonus for readers of Legacy of Leadership. Follow this link to access:
https://www.youtube.com/user/ideamanbob

Leadership under attack

Where were you when the planes struck the twin towers in New York City? What were you doing? What ran through your mind at that time?

There was a *noticeable* absence of national leadership for the first few days. During this vacuum, local leaders emerged, took responsibility, and stepped up to be counted. **This was leadership at its best!** When people with faults and challenges step up, put their fear behind, and do what is needed to lead, that is real leadership!

I was scheduled to speak in New Jersey a short time after 9-11. We rescheduled for December, and I flew into New York and arranged to view the devastation firsthand. What I saw on TV did nothing to prepare me for the sights, smells, and even the *taste* of being there in person. I will never get those images purged from my mind. This attack, and its aftermath, hit me on a very personal level.

The notes, pictures, and memorials for those who were lost impacted me the most. People just wanted to know if they were alive or not. I cried after reading the notes and the posters asking for information about their missing loved ones.

I'm brought in to chat about effective, dynamic leadership by organizations wanting to bring theirs to a higher commitment and focus. I love working with leaders as I know from experience when I reach them, engage them, energize them the whole organization is changed. I'd love to come and share a few ideas with yours. 1-**780-736-0009** or email me at **bhooey@mcsnet.ca**

WWII and the differences in 'leadership'
(Sept 1, 1939 – Sept 2nd, 1945)

Franklin D. Roosevelt, Joseph Stalin, Winston Churchill, Adolf Hitler, Benito Mussolini, Emperor Hirohito and **Hideki Tojo** were the main nation state actors in this second global war.

Each of them played a significant role in either the Allies or the Axis camp. Leaders or dictators depending on how you look at their roles in this historical global war. Each left a distinct legacy, some positive and some destructive to their respective countries. For this chapter, I want to primarily focus on the actions of one of them.

The most influential leader (Allies) during the war was **Sir Winston Churchill** who served as Prime Minister of the United Kingdom from 1940 to 1945, succeeding Neville Chamberlin. His forceful rhetoric and leadership inspired the United Kingdom and its colonies to resist the tyranny of Adolf Hitler, when his armies had all but conquered Europe, leaving the UK to fight alone. He kept working to bring the US into this battle for freedom behind the scenes.

Churchill's first speech as PM on May 13th set the tone for his war time leadership.

*"I would say to the House... that I have nothing to offer but **blood, toil, tears and sweat**. We have before us an ordeal of the most grievous kind. You ask, what is our policy? I will say: it is to wage war, by sea, land, and air, with all our*

might and with all the strength that God can give us; to wage war against a monstrous tyranny, never surpassed in the dark, lamentable catalogue of human crime. That is our policy. You ask, what is our aim? I can answer in one word: it is victory, victory at all costs, victory despite all terror, victory, however long and hard the road may be; for without victory, there is no survival."

Note: **Lend-Lease agreements** with the US gave Britain 50 American destroyers in exchange for free US base rights in various colonies. Roosevelt also set up a new method of shipping necessities to Great Britain. In essence, Roosevelt persuaded Congress that 'repayment' for all of this would be in defending the US. The Lend Lease program was formerly enacted on March 11, 1941. It truly made a difference!

The June 4th Dunkirk evacuation saved the British Expeditionary Force after the fall of France.

Churchill shared these inspiring words later that afternoon including a clear appeal to the United States.

*"We shall go on to the end. We shall fight in France, we shall fight on the seas and oceans, we shall fight with growing confidence and growing strength in the air. We shall defend our Island, whatever the cost may be. We shall fight on the beaches, we shall fight on the landing grounds, we shall fight in the fields and in the streets, we shall fight in the hills. **We shall never surrender,** and even if, which I do not for a moment believe, this Island or a large part of it were subjugated and starving, then our Empire beyond the seas, armed and guarded by the British Fleet, would carry on the struggle, until, in God's good time, **the New World**, with all its power and might, steps forth to the rescue and the liberation of the old."*

Essentially saying they would fight on until the United States woke up and joined the fight for freedom.

Additional history: Hitler attacked the Soviet Union on Sunday June 22nd, 1941, and another country was at war. Germany completed their conquest of France on June 25th, 1941. Italy entered the war on June 10th. Japan attacked Pearl Harbour on Dec 7th, 1941, and the war exploded across the planet with the US finally entering the efforts for freedom across the globe.

Critical dates to remember: May 7th, 1945, Germany surrendered. The Empire of Japan surrendered on August 15th, 1945, finally bringing this world conflict to an end.

Much has been written about WWII and its leaders. Perhaps it would benefit your leadership journey to research this history and the roles played by major actors on both sides of the conflict. Look at the actions of those on both sides of this conflict and learn accordingly.

My focus in briefly touching on some of this history was to outline how one person can become an influencer for good and lead the free world in defence of freedom. I call that, **"The Power of One"** in one of my keynotes. Perhaps you can be that person in your area of influence!

The *'Legacy of Leadership'* you choose is founded on those lessons and the interaction you've had with the people you were leading, as well as those who have invested in your own leadership journey. Leaders help other leaders grow!

"On very short notice Bob cleared his schedule and graciously presented at our meeting when the original Speaker was unable to attend. Last week Bob set the tone for our two-day leadership meeting and gave us all a motivational lift. His compassion and true interest in people were clearly evident, making him very credible. He shared some great stories, has a wealth of experience and knowledge and it was a pleasure listening to him. His down-to-Earth style makes it easier to retain the information presented. He also followed up with additional info and handouts, cementing his message of building bridges, not walls. Fantastic job, Bob, and thanks again!"
Barbara Afra Beler, *MBA, Senior Specialist Commercial Community, Alberta North, BMO Bank of Montreal*

"I just didn't have enough time!"

The harsh truth is *"we have all the time there is!"* Each of us has the *same* 1440 minutes in our day. What makes the difference is how we allocate and leverage those minutes. Or, how we allow others to misuse or abuse these minutes for us.

Despite a massive selection of seminars, notebooks, To Do lists, computers, and assorted electronic and paper organizers, we still find ourselves *too busy* and *overwhelmed* with commitments, obligations, and deadlines. **As leaders, being too busy to invest in working with, coaching, and leading your team can have drastic consequences for everyone, including us.**

We mean well, we really do! We even plan to buckle down and manage or schedule our time more effectively. Unfortunately, our human nature works against us, unless we make a disciplined effort to keep our lives and priorities on track.

The TRUTH – WE (not anyone else) are responsible for the gross mismanagement of our time and the amount of time WE allow others to waste. **We need to learn to say NO to the distractions and the actions that take us away from what is our most important functions, the best use of our expertise, skills, and energies.**

- What are we the *'best'* at?
- Why are we not focusing our energies on that *priority*?

We have all the *reasons* why we didn't use our time more wisely or should we say all the excuses. Sometimes the harsh reality gives us a wake-up call when we miss an important deadline because we procrastinated, overcommitted, or underestimated the time needed to finish a project and ran out of time. Sound familiar?

I've heard it said, *"Someone who lacks the will to say 'NO' will always be at the mercy of the time wasters"*. There are always people who will take your time. They will steal it, waste it, poison it, and rob you of the very essence of your life; unless you take control and decide for yourself who gets how much time and for what purpose. **Remember it's your time and it's your choice!**

Today, you can decide to fight and take back control of your time and life! It takes planning and discipline, but it can be done!

One effective technique learned to help recapture my time and life was to **set aside regular time to 'plan' future activities.** A few minutes spent planning each day, before starting, will save you hours! It is amazing what having a *daily focus* on the most important or critical activity can do to help free-up your time and stop saying yes as much!

Similarly, invest regular time weekly and monthly to layout and schedule your priorities (vs. prioritize your schedule), block out specific times, and allocate resources to reach your personal and professional goals. This will make a profound difference in your leadership, life management, and the results of your time investment. It did for me, professionally and personally.

Learn to **PLAN Monthly, SCHEDULE Weekly, and Lead Daily!**

Where are you on your personal timeline?

0_____*X*_____ 10

0=way far behind   10=doing very well

Take a moment and give yourself an honest evaluation of how well you are doing in managing yourself in relation to the time you have to lead, live, and create a lasting legacy. **Then ask yourself:**

- What obstacles stand in your way of moving closer to 10?
- What do you have to do or say no to doing to move your productivity and leveraged use of time closer to 10?
- When are you going to act?

38

Here is something adapted from our *'Running TOO Fast! Idea-rich strategies for the overwhelmed'* that might be a good investment of your time; especially, if you want to be a more effective leader in working with your teams.

For this brief exercise think through your daily interactions with the people on your team. Use the behaviour lists here (or adapt your own) and determine how much time (percentages) you invest on each one. In the next column put down the ideal allocation of time you would like to invest (again in percentages)

Behavior or action	% of time you invest now	% ideal time to invest
Directing		
Informing or explaining		
Clarifying or defending		
Persuading (nudging)		
Collaborating (teams)		
Brainstorming (envisioning)		
Reflecting (quiet thinking time)		
Observing (checking in)		
Disciplining (correcting)		
Resolving interpersonal conflicts		
Encouraging or praising		

Ask yourself:
1. Is there a gap between how I should invest my energy and time and how I actually invest it?
2. Are there actions/behaviours that take up too much of my time? Why?
3. Are there strategies I can employ that would move me closer to my idea investment of time and action?

Use the answers to these questions to help build a success strategy to leverage your time and actions for increased productivity: for you and your team. **When you take the lead, they will follow your example.**

Time to lead and succeed

Would an extra 8 to 10 hours per week of recaptured or repurposed time:
- **Make a difference in your workday or week?**
- **Make a difference in your productivity?**
- **Allow time for more training and delegating?**
- **Help you with career advancement?**

I frequently share these 60-second *time nudges* with my audiences and readers with the encouragement to explore them to see where they fit in their situation. Each works to liberate or create **5 to 30 minutes** a day by better use and leverage of your time and/or by eliminating time wasters. Some even more! Not all of them will fit your use, but you might glean an idea from each one. **First, a few foundational ideas.**

15-minutes a day works out to approximately 120 hours over a normal work year. 30 minutes a day is equivalent to 240 hours or a six- week work period. WOW! Perhaps, you can see where you might be able to better invest that recaptured time to grow yourself, your career, your team, or your business. Each can be explored and applied in less than 60 seconds. Good luck in your quest to regain control and leverage your time to be more effective in your life and career.

These small *seemingly insignificant* choices (minutes), when reclaimed and invested wisely over the course of your life, could give you the equivalent of an *advanced education* in a field of your choosing. Would this make a difference in your career path? **I would say YES!**

- For example: if we read an average of twelve pages a day (about 15 minutes), we could easily read 17-18 *self-study* books per year. Considering the North American average is **only ONE non-fiction book per year** – you might begin to see the competitive advantages of investing 15-minutes a day spent in self-study.

- We enjoy a definite advantage or an edge for success when we are well read. Reading BROADENS our experience and expertise and expands our possibilities. Sadly, statistics show that approximately **40% of North American adults are not *fully* capable of reading even their daily working material;** they are *functionally* illiterate. Investing as little as 15 minutes a day could effectively teach them the fundamentals of reading and make a major impact in their lives and employment prospects.

- The average North American drives about 12,000 miles (19,000 km) which translates into about 300 hours that can be leveraged for your growth. Turn your car into a mobile university by listening to top business leaders. Use your phone or MP3 player if you travel by transit for the same purpose. **Learn as you go is my motto.**

- Alternatively, these same ***seemingly insignificant*** choices could help us get into and stay in shape while tuning up our heart. I'm told just 15 minutes of cardio-vascular (aerobic) activity 3 times a week is all we really need to maintain a healthy body. Hmmm… INTERESTING! Only 15-minutes you say. …maybe tomorrow?

- Perhaps these ***seemingly insignificant*** choices could be spent or invested in personal meditation or spiritual contemplation, helping to bring your soul, mind, and spirit into balance.

- Maybe, these ***mini-moments*** could be shared exclusively with your family or close friends engaging in real, quality communication to create and build healthy life-long relationships?

"Don't waste time," wrote Australian pioneer **Arthur Brisbane,** ***"Don't waste it regretting the time already wasted… you have time enough left (for accomplishment and recovery) if you will but use it… while life and time remain."***

Your life and *time* management are in your hands. It is within your power to choose to invest it well for your benefit and the benefit of those you love and with those you lead. Or you can choose to let others rob you of your life's blood or squander it on useless pursuits.

It is your choice - and it's about your time!

A 60-second time nudge

Here are some quick reminders of simple, yet effective ways to be more productive and make better use of your time. If you are an extremely busy leader or manager, these will help. Are you serious about increasing your effectiveness as a leader and/or your income through sales, building your business and team, and finding ways to profitably create repeat buyers? **Learn and leverage my friend.**

Consistently and wisely using your time will allow you to free up time for face-to-face interaction with current and potential clients as well as working with employees to allow more time for the sales and management process. This *liberated* time can be leveraged by investing in equipping and motivating your team to grow and to win. Lead by example and get your team to apply these reminders to help them become more effective in their roles.

Strive for flexibility and balance

In the process of learning to effectively leverage your time, strive to find and maintain a flexible balance between your personal and business time. This is crucial to your long-term success! This is the only way you will find a *sensible* path that allows you to be productive, make the necessary changes needed to regain control of your life, and not burn out yourself, your colleagues, or your family members.

Strive for personal organization

Keep focused on what is important for you in each area of your life and career. Create your own *Focused Five* list where you outline the *single* most important action that will move that area (e.g., family, career, community, work, and self-growth) productively upward. Start each day with time focused on *planning* and then *schedule* what is truly of top value for that day. *Schedule your priorities!*

Remember: schedule around your personal energies and priorities to ensure the most important and creative activities are scheduled for that time when you are at your best. Time management is really a personal leadership choice to leverage your skills and priorities!

Configure your office for maximum productivity

Your on-site productivity starts with making sure your working environment is ergonomically designed and organized. Reduce the chances of repetitive strain injury (RSI) or long-term loss of energy by ensuring things are within easy reach and located where they offer you the best efficiency. I have learned the value of a well-organized workplace where I can easily access and find what is needed without needless wasted time. This one area can free up large blocks of time, a minute here and a minute there. That adds up over a day!

Learn and leverage using technology

With the advent of improved and cost-effective computers, printers, software, office networks, cell phones, etc. we finally have access to a group of tools we 'can' leverage to free up time. If you are looking for a competitive edge, you will find it by exploring and expanding your use of technology to systemize your business and reduce repetitive activities to a minimum. This is an area where you can design systems or access apps and programs which will allow you to free up and leverage larger increments of time. *Leveraging this area has allowed me to expand my ability to create programs and products to better serve my audiences and clients around the world.*

Use your website wisely

Smart business leaders and their teams are learning how to unleash the power of the Internet and harness the power of their websites by turning them into virtual assistants and sales agents.

Use your website as a client service tool, an information and resource base for potential and current clients. Create a website that can show your potential clients the depth and scope of your skills, services, and commitment to their growth, and success.

*Our **www.ideaman.net** website has been consistently revamped to do just that and it is paying for itself every year with client contact and contracts. We haven't even added the retail component yet.* ☺

*A few years back we revamped our **www.ideaman.net** website by asking some of North America's top experts to share their thoughts in **'A Creative Collection of Wisdom and Writing'** and have expanded the meeting planner section to offer assistance and free downloadable meeting and conference checklists, tips, and techniques from the experts.*

Also, visit our **www.BobHooey.training** website for information on our programs. Invest a few minutes checking these websites for informative articles on how to be productive in your leadership, career, and business.

Use your email effectively

Investigate ways of harnessing email to provide ease of access to clients, using autoresponders to answer common questions. Develop more effective ways of maintaining and initiating a true two-way communication with your suppliers, colleagues, employees, and clients. **Allocate specific times to access and respond to your email.** Use spam filters and create rules (which move regular emails from one source to a folder for later reading). Create contact groups for group emails and use autoresponders where applicable.

Get outside help

As you learn to leverage your time, do what other successful business leaders are doing in increasing numbers – find and engage outside help. Use the services of a virtual assistant. Look for ways to outsource repetitive and non-revenue or sales generating and marketing activities.

Perhaps you can work with a colleague to share the load or engage a part timer who is tasked to free you up for those high priority activities. This also creates more time for interaction with your team.

Leverage your marketing and promotion with assistance from others

If you are not marketing, you are marking time; and if so, it is only a matter of time until you are marked for failure. Can you team up to better reach your market?

Years back, I returned from our annual Canadian Association of Professional Speakers convention, after investing a weekend with 340 fellow speakers, trainers, and facilitators. One of the speakers reminded us that we were first a marketer, secondly a businessperson, and thirdly a speaker. This hit home with the volatile market following 9-11, the melt-down in 2008 and of course Covid-19.

Focus on the most productive form of marketing and promotion – your sales and service efforts

Each client you sell and then *successfully satisfy* can become a marketer/ or advocate for you and your services. Each client who continues to visit or do business with you can become a fan and champion on your behalf, *each employee too.* Ask for help in the other areas, such as networking, advertising, direct marketing, and public relations.

In 2006, I created a series of online promotional websites as a contribution to help some of my colleagues, along with myself, work together to better reach our potential clients. **www.AlbertaSpeakers.com** *was very successful over the years, as have the other regional websites we created.*

Leverage your time by better use of outside services

When you are busy and productively investing your time in the management, sales, and service process, make sure you work to minimize other activities that would distract you or deplete your time and/or energy. This one might be a more personal tip to free you up for more productive investment of time in your leadership role to train and equip your team to productively grow.

Look for ways to offload personal activities such as shopping services, personal assistants, cleaning services, etc. Use the Internet to its full advantage for services and products you need for your business and personal life as well. For example, many on-line office-supply services will deliver to your desk if your order meets certain levels. When you consider the time and expense of shopping personally, it just doesn't add up.

Plan monthly (or quarterly), schedule weekly, and LEAD daily!

I have been preaching this focused formula around the world for the last 22 plus years. And I am still learning. My experience and those of thousands of my readers and audience members has been to use this idea-rich success formula as a **strategic** *freedom or planning tool.*

- When you know what is truly important and are clear and honest with your values, you can say NO to things that do not fit and YES to those who do.
- Invest regular time either monthly or quarterly to think, reflect, dream, and then focus to gain freedom and to see your life become more productive, flexible, and balanced.
- Take the results of that process one step further and use that information to schedule focused time for specific activities on a weekly basis to systematically achieve your goals.
- *Personally, it frees me up to live and enjoy my life (on and off the job) daily.* I would hope it would serve that purpose for you.

This list of reminders or **time nudges** helps keep you on track as you strive to grow yourself and your team to the next level. Accomplishing this challenge will demand your continued *diligence* in getting the best results on investment (ROI) or *payback* from your investment of time and resources. Investing those resources and the time with your team will help you reach this level of success and the significance your desire.

More importantly, as you use these nudges to free up or recapture time (**5 to 15 min blocks**), make sure you know where you are going to reinvest this newly *found* time. Deciding in advance where you will *reinvest this liberated time* is a strategic move; one that will enhance your abilities to grow and to leverage your time for increased success and profitability. It will also allow you to inject a bit more fun in your life.

Strive for significance – lead on purpose!

A leader is a dealer in hope."

Napoleon Bonaparte

Japanese 23rd Psalm

When stress overwhelms you, the Japanese version of the 23rd Psalm can be very helpful...

The Lord is my Pacesetter, I shall not rush.
He makes me stop for quiet intervals;
He provides me with pictures of stillness,
Which restores my serenity.
He leads me in the way of efficiency through
calmness of mind, His guidance is peace.
Even though I have a great many things to
accomplish each day, I will not fret,
for His presence is with me.
His timelessness, His importance,
will keep me in balance.
He prepares refreshment and renewal in
the midst of any activity by anointing me
with the oil of his tranquility.
My cup of joyous energy overflows.
Surely harmony and effectiveness
shall be the fruit of my hours, and I
shall walk in the pace of the Lord,
and dwell in His house forever.

Author Unknown

As a leader, taking time to pause and reflect is a survival tool to help keep yourself centered and focused. This is how you succeed.

Productivity tips

A few years back, I had the pleasure of spending a couple of hours with **Darren Hardy**, *Publisher of 'Success magazine, What Achievers Read'.* Our discussion topic was how we could be more productive as leaders and entrepreneurs. This topic is very near to my heart, and I took copious notes as he shared his ideas and stories with us. I decided to pass along a few highlights from my notes and memory.

He challenged us to *say NO* more often and to narrow our focus and investment of time to the vital few functions that *only we* could do. He challenged us to cut back on where we *say YES* if we were serious about our productivity. He challenged us to move from **Reactive to Creative** and to delegate everything we could to free up time for pursuit of what is more vital in our lives. Bravo!

Darren's met and interviewed some of the world's top performers for his magazine. He went on to share examples of super-achievers who put some of these ideas into practice. **Sir Richard Branson** would work on only **3 strategic priorities** at a time. Apple founder **Steve Jobs** learned the power of working on **one BIG thing** at a time and would focus for 3 hours on his number one priority. **Warren Buffet**, on average, only took **1 of 100 deals** offered to him.

Darren suggested we should move from **Labour to Leadership**. He said everything *we DO* is keeping us from what we should be doing.

*This rang true for me as I had just presented in Ottawa at a national food and beverage conference for a group of club managers. I had challenged them to focus on what was the most **critical part of their role** and built on their expertise and experience. I had challenged them to invest time training their staff so they could delegate the less critical activities to them.*

He quoted **Kenneth Cole**, *"Success has less to do with what we can get ourselves to do and more to do with **keeping ourselves from doing what*** *we shouldn't."* I looked down at my *stylish* Kenneth Cole watch and smiled. This too hit home, as I tend to be excited about ideas and making them work. I say yes too easily, often, to ideas which don't move my career or business forward. Point well taken, Darren!

He quoted from an interview with **Steve Jobs** where Steve said, *"I am as proud of what we **don't do** as what we do."* He quoted from one of my favourite management gurus, **Peter Drucker** who said, *"There is nothing so useless as doing efficiently, that which shouldn't be done at all."* **Ouch!**

He challenged me again, as a leader and entrepreneur, to determine my vital few functions (that only I can do), my high impact priorities, and measurements to monitor and track my progress. *"This clarity would help in my quest to be more effective in what I do in my pursuit to help my readers and audiences grow and succeed."*

My plan is to do exactly that. I will be setting aside time to revisit my websites with an eye to adding more *clarity* in what I offer, and in what activities I engage in with my clients, colleagues and community. I pass along his challenge to you, my new friend and reader; in the hopes that what is shared in **'Legacy of Leadership'** will be a benefit for your growth and success as well as your life of significance.

Darren shared these points. He said, **don't mistake:**

- Movement for **Achievement**
- Activity for **Productivity**
- Rushing for **Results**

I've heard variations of these, perhaps you have too. I felt they were worth repeating. Wishing you all the success and satisfaction in becoming a more effective and influential leader in your field.

"Passion is energy. Feel the power that comes from focusing on what excites you."

Oprah Winfrey

How much is your time worth?

Have you ever taken a moment and thought about what your time is worth? Have you ever calculated your earning capacity on an hourly basis? It can be a great exercise in determining your worth, relative value, and earning contribution. It can also tell you how much each minute or hour you allow to be wasted is really costing you.

Let's figure out a typical time/value calculation. A typical year with 2 vacation weeks and 10 holidays leaves us with only 240-work days in which to earn our living. Assuming an average 8-hour workday this gives us **1920-potential work hours in a year.**

On the surface we'd simply take our Gross Pay and divide by the hours, e.g., $50,000/year would give us an average hourly rate of $26.04 per hour. In this instance each 15-minute block of **wasted time would be costing you $6.51. Work it out for your salary or earnings level to see the value of YOUR time!**

Let's take this a bit further, shall we? **In all honesty, would you say that you are able to get 8 productive hours in each 8-hour day?** Of course not! Honest feedback from quite a few of our North American audience members puts the 'true number' somewhere closer **to a generous 60% effectiveness on any given day.** I know some of you are saying, *"I only wish I had a 60% rate."* If that is true, then we really have only 1152-work hours in which to make our money. In the example above, each hour would now be worth $43.04 and each 15-minute block costing us $10.85.

Most of us would not deliberately waste a full day, but often let 15-minute segments slip away without notice or regret. This is one of the foundation points of success as a leader. **Take back your time and choose to invest it in your growth and in that of your team.**

Here are rough comparisons in our table for different dollar earning levels.

Annual Rate	Base Rate	Effective Rate (60%)	15-minute block
50,000/year	$26.04	$43.40	$10.85
100,000/year	$52.08	$86.80	$21.70
200,000/year	$104.16	$173.60	$43.40

Very interesting figures, aren't they? If you remain aware of what your time is 'really' worth it will help you keep an eye on the time wasters that creep into your life. Not that I put a monetary price on everything in my life; but it is good to know what my *investment* or *contribution* is worth. I invoice my no-fee clients (zeroed out) showing the real value of what I just *gave* them. This is as much for me as them.

After my dad died, I spent quite a lot of time with my mom before she passed away. It was probably the best return for my investment I've ever made – priceless! **I'd do it again in a heartbeat if I could.**

Our objective here is not to focus on the money, but to allow it to remind you how 'valuable' your time really is as a leader.

When working with executives and their teams on liberating time, we challenge them to focus on liberating (saving) **5-to-15-minute blocks** of time from their over-committed schedules. Their objective is creating at least one or more 15-minute block a day. Those 15-minute choices (segments) can be very valuable when focused on your more important priorities, one of which would be *working* with your teams.

Based on an improved age span of 85-years, we have **ONLY 31,046 days to LIVE!** Roughly 745,000-hours in which to live out our dreams, accomplish our life goals, create our legacy of leadership, and make an impact on our world and those with whom we share it. My bet many of you reading this are at least a quarter of the way down your path. Time is moving so quickly, and we have critical choices to make.

According to Goethe, **"One always has enough time, provided one spends it well."** What difference would that make?

Identifying and eliminating your time wasters

Over the years, we've asked our audiences about their time challenges and been able to identify their **25 biggest time wasters.** Here they are!

1. Telephone interruptions
2. **Failure to plan effectively**
3. Attempting TOO much
4. Drop-in Visitors
5. Socializing and daydreaming
6. Ineffective delegation
7. Travel (commuting)
8. Lack of self-discipline
9. **Inability to say NO!**
10. Procrastination - 'busy' work
11. Family concerns - distractions
12. Paperwork (where is the paperless office, they promised me?)
13. Leaving tasks unfinished
14. Not enough staff or personnel
15. Meetings (unnecessary or unproductive)
16. Confused responsibility (I thought you were going to do _____?)
17. Poor verbal and written communication skills
18. Inadequate controls, feedback, or progress reports
19. Inaccurate or incomplete information
20. Personal and corporate disorganization
21. Email, texts, etc. (great if targeted and used appropriately)
22. Management by CRISIS!
23. Cell phones, i-pads, and tablets (they can be great if used properly)
24. Television
25. Surfing the Internet, Facebook, Twitter, etc.
(Ok, I get caught up on it too!) www.ideaman.net

You may have some of your own time wasters, not on this list. Time wasters take away from your high priority time as an innovative, effective leader.

Take a moment to honestly appraise your life and leadership activities. Our audiences and leadership clients across North America have helped us come up with some novel approaches to help combat them.

Go through the time wasters list.

- Check off the time wasters you recognize (and remember the people who employ them against you) as draining your schedule and energy.
- Identify the major ones that are hurting your ability to successfully handle your leadership role.
- Decide to work on each one until you've eliminated or at least tamed it. Then move on to work on others.

Successful life and time management is a journey not a destination. As in any journey, the starting point is just as important as the destination.

One tip: don't try to deal with them all at once. Select the most important ones and work on them until you've beaten them. Then confidently tackle the next ones on your list. It may take some time, but, if you focus your energies, **you can take control!**

First ladies of leadership

My CAPS colleague and friend, **Patricia Katz** *is a woman I both admire and respect. Pat is the bestselling author of six books who also writes* **Pause***, a weekly online newsletter enjoyed by over 5000 subscribers. Through her presentations and publications, Pat helps leaders and organizations build more appreciative workplaces and more satisfying lives. She has served in many executive leadership roles in regional, provincial, and national professional associations. She was the first female President of CAPS National.* **www.PatKatz.com**

Time wasters – the dirty dozen
Developed for executives & administrative assistants.

For this *specialized* time management section, we polled people in support positions and asked them for their *dirty dozen* time wasters. We asked them to share in *confidence* and were amazed by what they told us.

This piece was originally focused for the assistants; but we realized it was helpful for their leaders and executives too. Perhaps you might catch a glimpse of where you, as a leader, are *not as helpful* in working with your assistants and teams as you would like to be. **Here they are.**

1. Lack of adequate planning
2. My boss's procrastination and lack of attention to making or following through on decisions.
3. Incompetent subordinates and co-workers *(This might be a training issue?)*
4. **My inability to say NO or set boundaries** *(Please be honest about workloads and setting priorities)*
5. Interruptions – drop-in visitors
6. Interruptions – telephone
7. Indecision
8. My procrastination
9. Forgetfulness
10. Meetings *(not needed or poorly organized)*
11. My challenge with perfectionism
12. Failure to delegate

Take a minute and think about these dirty dozens. **I challenge you to commit to being conscious of them as you work with your assistants.** Dedicated to my amazing *supportive* friends **Bridgette Dunphy, Irene Gaudet** and **Sandra Miko** who helped keep their respective leaders on track and on target. Ask your executive assistant to help you as you *continue* to work on them.

How to avoid *upward* delegation

One of the challenges leaders have are problems dumped into their laps. What makes it worse – some leaders actively take on challenges which need to be delegated to someone more qualified. Sadly, they allow their staff to **delegate upward** and add to their workload. This is the reverse of effective leadership.

Effective delegation is an essential leadership skill; one that is learned in the heat of over-commitment and the struggle to be productive. To avoid the *upward* delegation from subordinates and co-workers, be ready to ask them to answer the following questions *before* you and/or your immediate manager get involved.

1. Give me a clear statement of the problem, challenge, or idea.
2. What alternatives have you uncovered or researched?
3. What are the advantages and disadvantages for each of them?
4. What is your best recommendation to solve this challenge or to implement this idea and 'Why?' or 'What is the next step and why?'

It will take a while if you have been the **delegation-dumping** place for your office, but it will change when you set some *realistic* boundaries and challenge them to be responsible. You'll find that they will soon get the message: ***"Don't bring me a problem or challenge until you've done your homework and can help make a reasoned recommendation or decision."***

Another time waster is **useless** questions. Don't be afraid to make them do some homework.

When I served as District 21 Governor for BC's Toastmasters (1997-1998), I called the World Headquarters and asked a question. **Stan Stills** *took my call and was very gracious the first time. I remember him saying, "Bob, do you have your* **District Leadership Manual?**" *and continuing, "Let's see if we can find the answer to your question together." We did! He was very gracious, but I soon discovered I needed to do my homework first. Often, I found the answer in the book and only had to call when it wasn't specifically referenced or recorded.*

I'd suggest doing something like that with those who report to you or those co-workers who come to you as the office *'resource'* person.

4 questions that can help save you time:

Q1: Could the answer be found in meeting notes, files, or policies and procedures manuals?

Q2: Could another staff member or co-worker answer it?

Q3: Does it simply need a 'yes' or 'no' answer? Can that be handled by a quick phone call?

Q4: Is it a question that *really* requires your personal attention?

Tips on dealing with two top time wasters.

Dealing with Drop-In Visitors

This can be the toughest challenge in any office environment, more so with the advent of the open office layout and 'open door' policy. But you can get a handle on it if you are willing to do a little changing in your response to people and in how you interact as a leader.

Perhaps you could revisit the 'open door' policy and designate periods in the day when your door is closed; and people are told this is *'don't interrupt me unless it is a* **REAL emergency***'* time. Learn to develop defined signals and try to move them out of your office or work area. For example, stand up and walk with them in the direction of another area.

Take a strategic look at your office or work area. Are you sitting so you make easy eye contact with people as they pass by? Is there a natural conversation area or a place for them to sit or perch? Do you have a clock where it is easily seen? Perhaps you need to rearrange your office and workspace to help keep the distractions to a minimum?

Encourage your subordinates and co-workers to use 'save-up' files and not interrupt as often. Don't be afraid to tell them you don't have a minute to spare and ask if you can reschedule for later in the day or another time. You may find the problem got solved in the meantime.

Work to consolidate visitors and mini meetings to save on time disruptions. It is always easier to do several related things at a time than to jump back and forth between activities. Establish a *quiet time* and make sure your co-workers and subordinates know about it. *This can be transforming.* If applicable, get your immediate supervisor to buy-in as well. If you pitch it to him/her as a time in which you focus and deal with the creative issues on his/her behalf, you may find it an easier sell.

Leaders: Suggest that your assistants do a little horse-trading with a fellow assistant or co-worker to cover their/your calls and to run interference for you. Even 15-minutes of quiet, uninterrupted, focused time can be tremendously effective and productive.

Handling the phone-in time wasters

Here are a few tips that will help your assistant get a handle on the phone-in time wasters in your day. If you answer your own phone, you might get someone to cover for you on occasion or see where you can apply these tips we share with administrative or executive assistants.

Here is what we suggest as ways to be more productive:

- Screen your manager's calls and set up a hit list (always gets through, never gets through, or allow through at your discretion).
- Have your manager return calls where possible. Give him/her an outline of the question or message so they are well prepared!
- Don't ask open ended questions. Be specific and get the information needed for a quick call back by you or your manager.
- Use a call back system and consolidate your calls. Develop a script or agenda first! (This is a true time saver!)
- Avoid telephone tag: Make a specific phone appointment and/or leave a detailed voice mail.

Dirty Dozen *is excerpted is from Bob's "**Success Skills** for leaders, entrepreneurs, and those who support them."* When you apply these productivity tips you will be more productive and so will those who support you.

4 Ps of personal performance

I've had the privilege of traveling across North America, sharing my thoughts and seeing my **Ideas At Work** on how to regain control of your life, leadership, and time. I've been able to share with leaders, just like you, and heard your creative ideas and suggestions on how to effectively tackle the problems and time wasters we commonly face.

I hear leaders telling me, *"...life is good; but, out of control, over-committed, and with a blurring lack of focus on the important things and people in their lives."* Sound familiar?

Is there really an answer?

- Can we really take back control in this increasingly fast-paced world of Internet, cell phones, and other forms of **instant communication?**
- Can we balance our financial needs with our need for job, leadership, and family satisfaction?
- How do we balance our drive for personal and professional success with a need to **live our lives?**
- How do we create time to lead?

"Success is not about money; it's about what you feel about yourself, your life, your friends, and your loved ones," shares former *Success Magazine* CEO **Peter Morris**. *"My friend, **happiness, success, and enjoyment come from a balanced life,** where material and spiritual values are viewed in perspective. The most profound success derives from the consistent application of your natural skills and energy in work that constantly challenges you to expand your horizons. **Get a life!"***

The key here, as Peter said, **is the word balance and a sense of flexibility.** All too often we find our lives in an unbalanced situation.

This causes the negative stress on our lives, our families, and our career. **But how do we regain this balance?** The real secret is *simply* in how we portion out our time. We've experimented with new ways of looking at and blocking out my time. The results of this research are what we call the **4 Ps of Personal Performance.**

This planning process will, if applied wisely, help you re-focus your energies and resources in setting and achieving those worthwhile goals and the real desires of your heart. As a leader, please take heart, **you can gain freedom** by applying these techniques, along with the other ones we share in our programs and publications.

Our days are more effectively used when we focus, plan, or block out our time, based on what we call the **4 Ps of Personal Performance.**

In brief, **here they are.**

PEOPLE/PAY DAYS: Our success in life, leadership, and business is often directly related to our ability to relate and work effectively with other people. As leaders our success is very dependent on maintaining good working relationships with our co-workers, employees, employers, suppliers, competition, and, most importantly, clients.

Simply put, **a people/pay day** is one where the *major* time focus is on finding, building, and maintaining the relationships that are important in your life, leadership, and business. Investing time nurturing and augmenting these relationships can work miracles in team building, client loyalty, and business longevity. **Hint:** For the serious, effective leader, at least a part of each day should be invested in this quest to better understand, support, and equip your team to win!

POWER/PAPERWORK DAY: There are days when the deadlines, the commitments, and the process of running our business and career just must be our *major* time focus. Rightly so! The work must be done, the business must be managed, and the invoices and orders must be processed. **Power/Paperwork days** are the days in which **we set aside blocks of uninterrupted time** to focus on specific projects or obligations and work through to make sure they are completed properly and on schedule.

Days – when the work must be about the work – really do **WORK! Hint:** As a leader, this is where more effective direction and delegation come into play so you are freed up to accomplish your most important priorities and focus on your *vital* (only you can do) functions.

PAUSE/PLAY DAY: There are days when we need to regenerate, relax, take a break from our labours, enjoy our families, and sometimes daydream or even goof-off. Days, in which we have fun, not focused on building a business, or in pursuit of training that will advance our leadership careers. Maybe we take a **fun** course in something unrelated to what we do – just for the **joy of learning.** Maybe we take part of an afternoon off and sit quietly on a swing, or at the beach, watching the clouds as they slowly meander across the sky.

Pause/Play days allow us to reflect and refocus our energies, priorities, and resources; and help **make life worthwhile!** They are most effective in helping us regain control and in balancing our power and people days to maximize our effectiveness. **Hint:** Build this into your current leadership agenda. **Darren Hardy** told me, *"As leaders, we should get paid to rest, to pause. Our role is not defined by what we do, but often by what we don't do."* He suggested a process of **Sprint and Recover** where we work on one focused priority in 90-minute jam sessions and then allow ourselves to catch up or re-energize.

PLANNING/PREP DAY: These are day's allocated, monthly, or quarterly, to work **ON** your business or leadership, not **IN** the business. Days when the ***primary*** time focus is on strategic planning, analysis, and other functions of a long-range perspective. **Hint:** This is crucial as you seek to *liberate* time to become a more effective leader and help guide your team to more productivity and success.

Plan monthly, schedule weekly, focus, and lead daily!

That is not to say that you may have some weeks or days in which this isn't feasible, or you are working your way out of being over-committed. There are days when you will only be able to accomplish part of your goal to schedule a people day, a pause day, or a power day.

ReThink & ReTool Creativity

It is important to have a guideline to assist in effectively laying out your life and commitments. Having a guideline also helps keep you focused and working toward your optimum effectiveness. **Enjoy your life and choose to truly live, to effectively lead each day!**

Reminders to help you regain your balance and enjoy life.

- Just because you have the 'skill', **does not** mean you have the time! **Learn to say NO! This is one of your most important lessons if you are serious about creating time to lead.**

- Filtering your commitments through your life priorities can be a very effective tool against over commitment. **Ask yourself, "Is it 'really' important for 'ME' to do this?"** (Don't do – Delegate!)

- What activities can you eliminate, delegate, or ignore to free up time for the vital leadership activities and people you really value in life? **What's stopping you from being effective?**

- 5 minutes spent each day on pre-planning can save you hours in leveraged productivity. **Plan and then do!**

- 15 minutes daily invested in self-study or reading in your field of expertise can give you a major, idea-rich, competitive edge in your career. **A major investment that pays off big time!**

- Use your day timer or electronic organizer as a strategic planning tool to block out time for leadership development, family, planning, fun, commitments and deadlines, creative time, and time for yourself. **Control is a process of strategic planning**. It is a **foundation for success in living** and in seeing our lives become fulfilled and productive.

I welcome your ideas on how we can make it work even better. Email me at bhooey@mcsnet.ca

I've included Leadership videos as a bonus for our readers. Simply follow the link to access them on my YouTube Channel: *(80 leadership ones to date and more to follow)* ***https://www.youtube.com/user/ideamanbob***

Accountability - key to effective meetings

How often have you sat in meetings listening to *excuse after excuse* from people who didn't do what they said they'd do at the last meeting? People who are not prepared for the meeting or who haven't done their homework. How often have you led a meeting and heard excuse after excuse? Does it bug you? It sure does me!

One of the items I use to help *counteract* this frustration is a detailed *action list* (different than minutes) which summarizes what was agreed to be done, by whom, and by when. This accountability action list, kept and circulated in a timely manner to all in attendance immediately following the meeting, helps makes people take personal leadership and be more accountable for their actions or lack of action.

Two things will happen:

1) They will start doing more.
2) They will stop talking and over-committing.

Either way you win!

Here is a sample basic **Action List** form for your consideration:

Name	Action or commitment	Deadline	Done
Bob Hooey	Finish rewrites and edits	Dec. 30th	X
Irene Gaudet	Proof Legacy of Leadership	Jan. 14th	X
Bob Hooey	Send Legacy to printer	Jan. 19th	X
Bob Hooey	Promote Legacy of Leadership	on-going	

The secret to effective meetings is in a timely process of tracking and sharing accountability. That, coupled with setting your performance expectations high, can work wonders in any organization. This simple *leadership accountability tool* can be very powerful when used properly and publicly. Just as in the secret of success teams, group accountability can push us to complete that to which we commit. If the purpose for the meeting is important and vital to the success, growth, or other purposes of your organization or group, don't you think the follow through is *just* as important?

This is even more important in volunteer groups where people with individual agendas come together under a common banner. The challenge is to blend or re-direct those agendas to the common good. Then, having done that, to follow through and accomplish what has been discussed.

Don't be afraid to hold people accountable and set a higher standard. They will respond or they will leave you to accomplish that which is important. **Either way, you win!**

First ladies of leadership:

You'll see a few of these special women featured throughout the book. I wanted to encourage our women readers as so many of the more common leadership examples seem to be men. I believe we need both men and women who will take leadership in their area of interest. My late friend **Dianna Bowes** *was one of them in the Edmonton area. She had a passion for helping and inspiring baby boomer women. She had become a role model for so many in our area and a personal supportive friend to Irene and me.*

Dianna Bowes *was the founder of* **Fabulous @ 50** *and the editor of* **Be Fabulous! Magazine.** *Dianna was the winner of the 2011 YWCA Women of Distinction Award in the Turning Point category. She was a creative soul, who loved connecting people and embracing life. I still miss her.*

"Before you are a leader, success is all about growing yourself. When you become a leader, success is all about growing others."

Jack Welch

12 key strategies for 'Bringing out the BEST in people'

"Never, never, never, never, never give up!" was the sage advice of **Sir Winston Churchill** in answer to how he successfully led the British people to withstand the might of the Nazi war machine. When faced with a leadership challenge, remember his words and dig in… amazingly enough when you do, so will your team!

Alan Loy McGinnis wrote **'The Time Trap'** in the last century about bringing out the best in people. It was well-received and gained exposure and acceptance among *progressive* leaders at that time. I've reflected on what he outlined and had his **'12 Rules'** sitting on the wall above my desk as this chapter was originally written. They served as a *visual guide* and reminder of their importance in leading and coaching the people, *like yourself*, with whom I have the privilege of working with across North America and, more recently, across the globe.

If you are *committed* to being an effective leader, perhaps they should be sitting somewhere close, so they are not far from your mind's eye. They are included, along with my own reflective thoughts, for your **inspiration, information, and illumination**.

Expect the best from the people you lead

See them performing at their best, even when they are struggling. People will often rise or fall to the level of our expectations and our coaching. See them as they could be, not as they are! Don't limit them by expecting or accepting less than their best. You owe it to them to set realistic, but challenging expectations. You can help them reach these as their coach, cheerleader, or champion. This can be a large challenge when you are a leader faced at working with what seems to be a dysfunctional or fractious team. Your saving grace can be keeping your eye and those you lead on the ultimate or shared goal.

For example, **General Eisenhower** *had the challenging role of being the supreme commander in the liberation of Europe during the Second World War. He faced an enemy who was well equipped and motivated to win. He also faced the challenge of working with warring factions within the Allied ranks. He persevered and went on to help us win.*

Make a thorough study of the other person's needs

Each person on your team is an individual with specific skills, talents, strengths, weaknesses, needs, and dreams. Investing the time to get to know them makes it easier to lead and direct them for mutual success. Investing time in understanding and getting to know them also builds strategic bonds which can build bridges to the success and positive performance of them and your team.

Weak leaders lead from the surface. Strong leaders dig deep to learn what best motivates those they lead. They know where to best challenge and direct their skills for success. This allows them to best direct and use the talents and skills of their entire team.

Establish high standards for excellence

Leaders *ultimately* fail when they accept mediocre results or neglect to set challenging standards. As mentioned previously, don't fail your team by allowing them to be *just* ok in their roles.

People will amaze you when you set the bar higher and lead by example. There are valid examples where good enough is appropriate. However, we settle for *seconds* (leftover's) when we could have reached higher, dug deeper, and been more successful. Be realistic but be ready to push past the comfort zone into the winner's zone. The example and standards you set and accept as a leader will determine the growth and success of your team.

Create an environment where failure is not fatal

Mistakes are a *natural part of life* and taking risks means occasionally you fail. If your team feels supported and encouraged, they will begin to take risks and move past their **comfort zone into the winners' zone**.

Help them learn from the lessons of any mistakes and move ahead with energy to face the next challenge. Help them stretch and grow, knowing that they will make mistakes in their journey, as you did!

I remember having one of the clerics in my Tehran, Iran audience take me aside to talk about this. He talked about being a martyr for God. I got more concerned as we talked.

Eventually I said, **"Seems like we are both saying we want our people to take risks."** *He nodded, and I quickly said goodbye and walked away. Whew!*

If they are going anywhere near where you want to go, climb on other people's bandwagons

A *wise* leader is open to letting his team set the pace and direction, provided it takes them along the path towards the eventual goal set by the leader. In this case, you as the leader can become the cheerleader and coach, helping them move along more successfully. *I have found team members had great ideas and their creative input moves us successfully forward.*

Sometimes, however, you need to be honest and realize that people are not going the same direction or share the same values as you. In that case, redirect them or let them go and stay your own course. Be courageous enough to realize that you can follow your own path. Others who share your values will follow.

Employ strategic models to encourage success

This goes to the *heart* of leadership by example. Make sure this is modeled in your own life and in the lives of those you promote and delegate to succeed.
When your team sees it working in your life and actions, they will be more open to allowing change in their own lives and performance.

Recognize and applaud achievement

People do not work *simply* for money. In fact, most of the lists compiled show money much lower on the chart of motivators. Each employee or team member has his or her own needs, desires, and drives. Know them so you can strategically employ them.

Two of those needs, deep inside each of us are:
1) The need to feel *appreciated* and important.
2) The need to feel *included* in the process.

As a leader, the most effective thing we can do is to recognize achievement and effort from those we lead and to share and applaud their achievements. Often small, genuine recognition activities will be more effective than fancy reward programs. The point is to make sure you see what they are doing and let them know you appreciate it. **Hint:** Make sure any recognition is relevant to their needs and desires.

Employ a mixture of positive and negative reinforcement

We understand it is a good thing to provide praise and positive reinforcement in our team members' efforts. This affirms their actions and encourages them to move ahead. Praise in public.

It is also necessary, at times, to apply the opposite tactic when one of them is doing something detrimental or self-defeating in the fulfillment or follow-through of their role. Letting them know what is **NOT** acceptable is part of a leader's role. We can do it nicely but do it we must; if they are to grow and maximize their potential. Correct in private as your goal here is to help them, not embarrass them.

Appeal *sparingly* to the competitive urge

Each of us has a natural competitive edge. If used wisely, competition for personal growth and success can be a great tool to much higher achievement. However, it has its *dark* side in allowing divisive actions and negative attitudes to creep into a team environment. Focus on the *team accomplishment* and mutual win. Encourage each team member to compete for higher standards and personal skill development.

Place a premium on collaboration

This is where team 'works' and where effective leaders learn to pull people from diverse backgrounds, agendas, and experiences into an effective working unit.

Brainstorming is one way of effective collaboration and team building, allowing each team member to build and draw on the brainpower of another. What you are looking for is adding value vs. tearing down or unproductive criticism and negativity.

Build into the group an allowance for storms

It is not always smooth sailing as a leader. Surprise, surprise! Storms, difficulties, challenges, detours, and disasters can strike when you least expect them.

When we were sailing to Japan from Hawaii in summer of 1988, we encountered what the Japanese later told us was a 'baby' typhoon. I'm sure glad it didn't reach puberty! ☺ Our captain was an experienced sailor and former US Coast Guard Captain. The other two crew members had deep water experience and had encountered similar storms (but not typhoons).

I had never experienced anything like this as most of my sailing was near coastal or island areas! I was more than a bit nervous, more so when we tipped the boat and almost sank. ☺

"As we look ahead into the next century, leaders will be those who empower others."
Bill Gates, co-founder of Microsoft

68

Captain John's commanding leadership, along with the hands-on experience of **Phil** and **Dave** helped us survive this life threatening super-natural phenomenon. We fought the storm for over 13 hours before reaching safer sailing. We dealt with it as needed to survive and to gain our port of Kobe, Japan.

As a leader, you need to build in allowances for these *speed bumps, storms,* and *detours* in your team's progress and have plans in place to cover each potential challenge. Sometimes you need to step in and help them weather the storm.

Take steps to keep your own motivation high

You are 'on' as a leader all the time. This means people will be looking at you and taking their cue from you. It also means you need to keep your personal motivation high and maintain a positive outward attitude. This means you may need to find a trusted advisor or coach with whom you can discuss your challenges in private.

Letting your negative feelings show can be devastating to your team. They look to you as being confident, clear in focus, and consistent in action and follow through. Don't disappoint them.

Understand and learn to apply these basic keys (rules) of the leadership road to smooth out your path and make it easier for those who follow you to successfully walk in your footsteps.

"Let me assert my firm belief that the only thing we have to fear is fear itself. We look forward to a world founded upon four essential human freedoms. The first is freedom of speech and expression. The second is freedom of every person to worship God in his own way. The third is freedom from want. The fourth is freedom from fear." **Franklin D Roosevelt**

What makes them the BEST?

"Leadership at its 'best' is about developing other strong leaders." **Bob 'Idea Man' Hooey**

Each year companies from across Canada apply to be judged for this challenging designation. Each year a few make it, some re-qualify, to be named as **Canada's 50 Best Managed Companies**.

Sustained success in any field is built on a solid foundation of strategic, inspirational leadership. Leadership sets the pace, fuels the growth, and equips and motivates the team to succeed. Leaders cannot accomplish this alone, but they are the key in its accomplishment. What have you done to lead, assist, and motivate your team to succeed today?

I've had the privilege of working with senior executives from this well-deserved group of companies. I've seen first-hand their leadership in action and the positive, profitable, and productive results it inspired.

Here are four crucial areas with twelve focused points created in a keeper card when one of the companies I worked with achieved this goal. We had a challenge drawing down to these 12 pivotal points so we could create a business sized laminate card for each of their nearly 6,000 employees across Canada as well as those who attended the award ceremony.

They shared these points that evening in their continued **Striving for Excellence** focus.

Building
- Bridges not barriers or boundaries
- Profitable client and supplier relationships
- Success via long term vision and value

Empowered employees
- Putting their enthusiasm and energy to work
- Committed to excellence in serving our clients
- Providing inspired 'by example' leadership

Strategic
- Thinking in focus, value, and action
- Recruiting and promoting the 'right' leaders
- Alliances with strong leaders and companies

Training
- Employees to succeed in and on the job
- Initiative and innovation in client service
- Executives in honing their leadership skills

Perhaps you can leverage these points or create your own. Having some simple points of focus will help you keep on track in your efforts to better serve your team, enhance your leadership, and build a successful team and organization.

"The credit belongs to the man (woman) who is actually in the arena; whose face is marred by dust and sweat and blood; who strives valiantly; who errs and comes up short again and again; who knows the great enthusiasms, the great devotions, and spends himself (herself) in a worthy cause; who at the best knows in the end the triumph of high achievement; and who at the worst, if he (she) fails, at least fails while daring greatly ..."

Theodore Roosevelt

I love this quote and had it on my office wall for many years. It challenged me to act on my ideas **(Ideas At Work!)** It goes right to the point of being an active leader who is willing to step up and step into the arena of life. **We lead best when we live our life as an epic adventure!**

A guide to the care and feeding of new employees or volunteers... the first 90 days

"You may have the loftiest goals, the highest ideals, the noblest dreams, but remember this, nothing works unless you do."
Nido Qubein, President of High Point University

Adding someone new to your team or staff is very *much like* a first date. Both parties are a little anxious, eager to please, and with mixed expectations. Sometimes it can turn out the same way as a first date! ☺ However, there are a few timely and helpful guidelines.

As an employer or team leader, you have a lot riding on the decision to hire or recruit. Aside from money and time invested, your reputation and organization/company are on the line, along with the working relationships already established within your current team.

It can easily cost you up to six months wages to train a new employee, in the extra time spent supervising, training, and in lost time or costly mistakes. More so bringing volunteers up to speed as you learn together. Invest wisely!

Each new hire or volunteer has some risk, in the time invested to learn new products or services and build a new client base. Wouldn't it be a clever idea to work at creating a successful partnership that allows both parties to win? With the major investment of 'time', both parties would be open to working together in making it a successful partnership.

One of the basic foundations for growth and success in any working partnership is to be clear and realistic in laying out the new role and its related responsibilities. Nothing frustrates as much as not knowing what to do or looking dumb when you have missed something that *"everyone else knows but forgot to let you in on the secret".*

72

Being realistic in laying out a *timeline* for learning and assimilating before establishing firm goals is important too. This needs to be tailored to the expertise, experience, and aptitude of each new hire.

Leaders, tough as it seems, *"You treat them all the same by treating them differently"*. Most parents have already learned this valuable lesson.

As the employer or team leader, you need to work to establish an environment to encourage asking questions as well as asking for help. This saves time, frustration, and mistakes. It helps build a positive relationship that will make your innovative partnership grow. **To get the most out of your latest hire or volunteer, follow these hints.**

Define the position carefully

What are the new hire's responsibilities – in *every area* of their position? To be effective, what skills, knowledge, and attitudes must be displayed? Be as clear and specific as you can. It will set the tone and foundation for eventual success for yourself and your recruit. Doing this also helps you focus on what you want from this recruit. This will help you guide yourself and them to better success.

Hire or recruit selectively

Hiring or recruiting people who have existing training or expertise reduces your time and resource investment. Investigate who trains people with the skills you need and call them.

When I was part of the management team working to open the first two BC Home Depots, we did this. We looked for people with a proper attitude (customer service) who had the basic skill sets or knowledge we needed. We would then train them on the job to be more knowledgeable in their particular department.

Be specific about where each employee or volunteer needs improvement

Can the lack of performance be fixed through training? Perhaps! Sometimes it's motivation or a personal problem. Clearly communicate these areas and offer your support. Don't be afraid to spell out the consequences if the deficiency in performance remains unchecked. At this point in the process, it is your responsibility to help them learn in place and be able to perform.

Provide on-going support and encouragement

Assist employees in selecting and undertaking personal training and professional development. Investing in their growth often returns large dividends. This is where you risk investing time now for better performance and productivity at a future time.

Measure and communicate results

Do not be afraid to hold your staff (paid or volunteer) for training outcomes, reasonable expectations, and responsibilities that have been well communicated. Check to see if training has reduced or eliminated the employee's or volunteer's skill or knowledge deficiency. This is where you, as the leader, must be clear in your communication and firm in your expectations to help them grow.

Check to see if the staff member/volunteer is equipped and empowered to make a better contribution to your organization or company. Do this in a timely and constructive manner.

Set aside regular, uninterrupted, time to discuss training and performance issues. Do not wait until the probationary (typically 90 day) period has expired to ask for changes in performance or to offer critiques; by then it is often too late. Work with them *in the moment* and/or on a regular basis so they know how they are doing and how to do it better.

If you are *selective* in whom you recruit or hire and are *diligent* in the time you invest together, you will see your investment pay handsomely in contributing and productive employees who add value to your firm and use their new skills for everyone's benefit.

One training tip would be to *standardise* as much of your business/organization, its procedures, processes, systems, and special challenges or activities as possible. This will be an immense help in getting new recruits up to speed. This is also a wonderful way to keep existing team members current, engaged, and focused. Ask for their help with this.

Make sure training is a work in progress. Enlist and empower your current team members in its creation and upkeep. Many organizations have moved this work-in-progress on-line to allow it to be amended as needed. This is a great way to build and maintain your working relationship and foster a sense of partnership among team members.

What happens if you are a seasonal employer, or this is a project action team, and your training time is much shorter?

How do you make the best of your training time and maximize your investment? How do you hire skilled staff? This is a crucial factor to keep in mind when you are interviewing prior to hiring. Making sure you pick those open to work and learn on the job is important; but after they are on board then what?

Jeremy Pinder from Australia said, *"Because I am in the recruitment business, I get calls on a regular basis asking,* **'Where can I find good staff?'** *It annoys me, but I just tell them that they are asking the wrong question. What they should be asking is,* **'How do I take the staff that I've got and make them better?'"** Good change of perspective with great results!

My friend and fellow speaker **Bill Marvin, CSP - The Restaurant Doctor** from Washington had this to say, *"You already have the kind of people you need. If they are not performing up to your standards, whose fault is it? They asked for a job, you gave it to them! You need to look at who is responsible for performance."*

Bill shares, *"If you place the burden on the staff, you are at their mercy. It is not going to change until they change. However, if you accept that your job, maybe your most important job, is staff development, then training and performance become YOUR responsibility and that you can do something about!"*

From a business perspective, your challenge as leaders, managers, and employers is to seriously look at the cost of having untrained or poorly trained staff in lost business or unhappy customers.

How much is each client worth to your business? As employees, your career is enhanced by better care of clients or customers.

In our client service seminars, we have our audiences work this value out. Then we hit them with the truth — based on proven statistics, each unhappy customer costs you the value of **'that'** *number multiplied by sixteen. The unhappy customer doesn't return, he tells at least 10 people about his unsatisfactory experience on average and doesn't tell the 5 people about a happy experience as would be expected. Ouch!*

Spending time and money in protecting your investment and the reputation of your business is time well spent.

It can be tough to look at investing time training people who may only be with you for a season. But if you are honest with yourself, you will see it is an investment that *must* be made if your business is to grow and flourish.

Taking advantage of available or pre-packaged training systems can be a good investment. Do not reinvent the wheel. Check out what is available from national, regional, local agencies and correspondence training programs. There are programs for employers and employees in various industries and they can be adapted to your specific team needs.

Looking for ways of working together would be a good idea too!
How about working with owners in similar businesses to cooperate on staff training? I'm sure you can see reasons to justify joining forces in training staff in areas of common interest. It may be a bit of a challenge to get past the normal competitive urges. Good luck in your training efforts; your success depends on the decisions and actions you make in this regard.

"Knowing is not enough; we must apply.
Willing is not enough; we must do."
Goethe

Seize The Day

"Seize the day! Give it Life,
for it will come no more.
See the beauty amidst the strife,
And be happy forever more.

Live for today!
And you will improve tomorrow
and make a happier yesterday.
But live for tomorrow
or long for yesterday,
and you will have lost...
As your life drifts away.

Each day well lived, each seed sown
Looks after the future,
so we can blossom...
Like the flowers have grown.

Seize the day! Seize it now!
Be grateful you have it all,
and every night
as you lay to rest...
you may say:
I am happy, I gave it my ALL."

Sean M. Kelly

A reminder to make sure each day is fully lived – leadership is best
lived as an adventure and each challenge is both embraced and enjoyed.

Heart to heart – how to lead and inspire!

"To be a leader means willingness to risk – and a willingness to love. Has the leader given you something from the heart?"
Hubert H. Humphrey

My friends and readers I have yet to meet, it is my privilege to share with you some of what I am learning about leadership and to further share what is in my heart.

By this time tomorrow several thousand people, many of them young people, will attempt suicide. Too many by far will *succeed*. Too many will die of alcoholism or drug related causes, confront their first mental collapse, suffer a heart attack or stroke from excess stress, or be pried needlessly from their mangled vehicles. **This, too, is a part of our legacy**.

Why? Many of them are already *dead* and just looking for a way to make it permanent. They have lost hope and drift helplessly, *leaderless* through life. Thousands of our fellow citizens are confined to self-constructed prisons of pity, despair, and defeat; dungeons of self-depreciation – not realizing that THEY alone hold the key to their own freedom.

In 1988, when my first marriage and then later my business went south, I took up residence there, myself, *for a short while*. But though I am occasionally temped to visit, following the death of my parents in 1999, following the aftermath of 9-11, or the crash of 2008, or the recent Covid-19 shut down, I don't venture there anymore.

Somehow along the way, our friends and fellow citizens lost their way, lost their desire for a better life, and saw their dreams destroyed as they watched *helplessly*.

Maybe you are experiencing this challenge in your life? Abused, disheartened, our friends no longer laugh or enjoy life. They've stopped fighting, surrendered their self-esteem, bankrupt their potential, and have given up. They've resigned themselves to a life of *mediocrity* and desperation. Does this sound familiar?

We cannot leave them dying by inches!

Many years ago, I grew to realize that any *real inspiration,* and any *real leadership*, must come from the heart. It is only *effective* when it is received and embraced by another heart – that is **heart to heart**.

Like life, inspiration and leadership are precious! Like water on a burning desert, it is sprinkled on dry souls, to moisten parched lips unable to speak, to free a unique voice; to experience, firsthand, the miracle of resurrecting oneself from a *living death*.

If we were sitting in Starbucks, Second Cup, Tim Horton's, or some other coffee shop we could undoubtedly share for hours about the abuses, afflictions, hardships, or challenges we each face. I would, however, like to draw your attention to a much more devastating abuse, a common denominator to our deadly despair – *emotional abuse*.

How many of us have encountered the **Dream Killers**? Those sometimes, well-meaning people, perhaps family, who judge us or try to kill our dreams, our futures by criticizing us – *for our own good?* Some are in positions of authority, who, as the *expert,* tell us why it won't work. They chip away at our self-esteem and would extinguish our pilot light of hope – to see us shackled into conforming, mediocre lives of defeat (like theirs).

How, then, can we defend ourselves against this emotional abuse, especially from those we love and trust?

Let's explore how each of us can take a *real leadership role* in this battle for the mind and soul of our country and by *leading by example* to inspire those around us.

We live in one of the world's greatest places (North America) and yet our *ships of state* flounder in seas of red ink, tossed about, its citizens abused, abandoned, and driven slowly onto the rocks of depression and destruction. North Americans are losing hope. They are tired of *uninspired* officials who do not lead, who have no vision, and who pander to us rather than telling us the truth, who squander our future.

REAL LEADERSHIP, serious leadership, is about compassion, conviction, and courage.

Compassion is drawn deep from a caring heart, fortified with *conviction* of purpose. It is established by the *courage to lead*, stand *alone* as necessary in the achievement of a worthy cause or in battling an injustice. Isn't real leadership about finding the courage to follow your own dreams, despite the challenges you face seeking them?

Many of us suffer hurts, a psychic wound that saps our spirit, hinders our leadership potential, and drains our day-to-day lives. That is a part of life. **How well we live is related to how well we deal with these hurts.** As individuals, these hurts, unresolved, can negatively impact and impede our leadership.

If I could, I would cup each face gently with my two hands, as my mom used to do, look deep into your eyes, into your soul and gently speak to that hurt.

- You are a miracle of God's creation!
- Your dreams have purpose and value!
- Your dreams are still within your grasp!
- It is never too late to start or start again!
- God loves you and believes in you! I believe in you!
- God has given you all the talent and desire you need to succeed!
- There are people just waiting to help you succeed, you need only ask!
- You can *still* do it! There is *still* time for you!

I DARE YOU!

Physically, I am not able to do that. Some of you reading this book will be across the country or even on a different continent.

Can I *learn* to take control, to continue taking responsibility and exhibit leadership in my own personal battles? Perhaps, in that, to give some inspiration to those I encounter along the way. (*That was my personal challenge, as originally shared in this speech, in 1992. That is a worthy challenge for me this year and the next too!*)

What I am attempting to say, what I am attempting to learn is, "*We don't have to have it all together to lead or to inspire.*" **Leaders do not have to be perfect to be productive or effective.**

We begin to do so when we begin to care! Inspirational leadership can be as simple as a word of encouragement shared in passing; in openly sharing one's struggles and lessons or in being honest enough to admit our personal neediness and in being willing to ask for help.

There were times I arrived at the place I was to speak, figuratively dragging my butt. I have been repeatedly inspired by my fellow professional speakers and Toastmasters to place my hurts aside, to give each audience my best, my all, each time I speak. It works!

Together we can take personal leadership in this crusade to end and abolish this emotional abuse, banish forever the dark tyranny of our soul. Let's begin today! Leadership begins with you! It begins with me!

- *Never again* will we allow the needless sacrifice of our individual dreams for the *common good*.
- *Never again* see our potential bowing, prostrate before a monument to mediocrity.

My friends, the prison doors are open, they were never locked. I challenge you to alter your attitudes, to purge the poisons of pessimism from your minds, and to dare to dream again. Capture the moment, if you will, your permanent dream. Hold it clearly in your mind's eye, burn it again deeply into the fabric of your soul.

Can you see it? **Can you see yourself achieving it? I can!** Are you willing to share it, to live it, to champion its cause? I dare you to lead, to dream, and to inspire those who watch you hoping for a glimpse that they, too, can follow your lead.

To sum up my thoughts

When, at first, we realize the truth about ourselves and our dreams, *then*, we begin to see the truth around us. When we speak in defence of the truth, *then*, we begin to really *lead* in this fight for human dignity.

When we open our hearts, *then*, we begin to truly inspire and lead those around us. **Canada needs your leadership!** North America needs your leadership. The world needs your leadership. I need you!

I challenge you to join me in leading this crusade and creating a significant legacy of leadership. I invite you to make this leadership commitment, where you are sitting now. Let us serve notice that we are willing to dream, to lead, and to forge our lives into real *heart to heart* inspiration. **I dare you!**

Note: *This piece was originally crafted as a speech given back in January 1992. Its message is just as timely 32 years later. I challenge you to make sure you connect with those you lead from a heart position and not just a head position. If you would inspire them to move and act on what you ask – ask from the heart.*

Leadership productivity tips

- If it can be done in 2 minutes or less – *DO IT NOW!*
- **Create lists:** Project, next action, waiting for, **STOP** doing, calendar deadlines, and someday!
- **In-box strategy:** Get to the bottom each day. Deal with one item at a time. Don't put it back.
- Use the 6 Ds **Discard, develop, delegate, delay, deposit or DO IT!**
- **Read and study at least 15-minutes each day!**

History tends to repeat itself

My wife, Irene, is Ukrainian, with her grandparents on both sides emigrating to Canada in search of a better life. So, we have watched (Feb. 2022) with concern as Putin's murderous forces un-righteously attacked schools, hospitals, and day care centers in an unsuccessful terror campaign to weaken the will of the Ukrainian people. His troops killed and wounded civilians without any regard. PS: He is losing!

We watched with amazement when they were bogged down, ran out of gas, saw 1000's of Russian conscripts deserting the battle and Ukraine more than holding her own and winning against a 'superior' foe.

Perhaps a bit of **historical background** will help frame this chapter on contemporary leadership.

A 1922 treaty between Russia, Ukraine, Belarus, and Transcaucasia (modern Georgia, Armenia, and Azerbaijan) formed the Union of Soviet Socialist Republics (USSR). Lenin took control of the government. At its height it comprised 15 republics: Armenia, Azerbaijan, Belarus, Estonia, Georgia, Kazakhstan, Kyrgyzstan, Latvia, Lithuania, Moldova, Russia, Tajikistan, Turkmenistan, Ukraine, and Uzbekistan. Stalin rose to power in 1924 and ruled by terror, enacting brutal polices that would leave millions of citizens in the USSR dead. Stalin realized an opportunity toward the end of the 2nd World War and rapidly took control of a number of countries to expand the Soviet Union. He and his successors ruled with an iron fist and people learned to live under a dictatorship and with the threat of atomic war with the west.

In 1949, the US, Canada and its European Allies formed the North Atlantic Treat Organization (NATO) as a political show of force against the USSR and its Eastern Bloc (Warsaw Pact) alliance. An unsuccessful coup by hardliners in the Communist Party sealed the Soviet Union's fate by diminishing **Gorbachev's** power leading him to resign in August 1991. **Boris Yeltsin** took power. At that time Ukraine severed its ties to the Soviet Union, providing a coup de grace. Ukraine was a cornerstone of the Soviet Union, home to the Black Sea Fleet and much of the Soviet Union's agricultural production, military, and defence industries.

Since declaring its independence in 1991 with the dissolution of the Soviet Union, Ukraine has sought to establish itself as a sovereign state while looking to more closely with Western institutions, including NATO and the European Union.

Pivotal note. December 1999 saw the resignation of Boris Yeltsin putting **Valdimir Putin** in place as Acting President of the Russian Federation. He has steadfastly schemed to remain in power and saw the Ukrainian direction as a direct threat. With the loss of other Soviet block countries, he became focused on trying to rebuild the former Soviet Union in his own warped image.

Russia annexed Crimea ('rescue' operation) in 2014 and began arming and supporting Donbas separatists. The fight continued. In February 2022 Putin directed a full-scale Russian invasion of Ukraine set on toppling the Western-aligned government led by Volodymyr Zelenskyy.

Ukrainian President Volodymyr Zelensky is a former comedian, actor and politician who is serving as the 6th (current) President of Ukraine since 2019.

At times a leader is revealed during strife and chaos, and this is certainly the case in Ukraine and the inspirational journey he has led. His leadership journey is a lesson for all of us.

Ukraine has extended its ties with NATO and the European Union over the years leading up to the 2022 invasion and is seeking to eventually gain full EU and NATO membership. That, we think, drove

Putin crazy and sparked, in part, his ill-advised, ill-planned and ill-equipped invasion of independent Ukraine.

The unprovoked, *murderous* invasion of Ukraine has left over 100,000 Ukrainians wounded or killed, many of them women and children. Even more than double that number of Russians have been killed or wounded. Over 8 million refugees left the country and millions more were displaced with the fighting. Russia's missile and drone strikes continue to flatten cities and civilian infrastructure throughout the country. Putin's strikes murder Ukrainian civilians at will!

Yet, Russia's *so called* overwhelming armed forces have been bogged down, and in many cases beaten/driven back by committed Ukrainians.

President Zelensky has risen to become the inspiration for millions in his country. His leadership success has led to a strengthening of NATO and new nations seeking membership. He has inspired nations around the world to lend their support to his band of patriots in their righteous fight to push back and defeat Russia. In essence, he has become **the leader of the free world**. With continued support and re-supply, they will eventually force Russia to retreat and leave Ukraine.

A few Zelensky quotes to support that:

"Nobody is going to break us: we're strong, we're Ukrainians."

"Ukraine is the heart of Europe, and now I think Europe sees Ukraine is something special for this world. That's why the world can't lose this something special."

"We do not hold out, we fight, and our nation will fight to the end. This is our home, we are protecting our land, our homes. For the sake of our children's future." *(Sounds like Winston Churchill during the battle of Britain to me.)*

"To all the countries of the former Soviet Union – look at us, everything is possible."

When he was offered a way out to safety, his response: "I need ammunition, not a ride."

"When you attack us, you will see our faces. Not our backs, but our faces."

As I said, leaders can be revealed in the heat of battle and crisis. This is certainly the case in Ukraine. President Zelensky and his people serve as an inspiration to rest of the free world that good can triumph over evil.

Note: Things are un-ravelling in Russia. Tens of thousands have protested his illegal invasion, many of them being thrown in prison, and some giving their lives. Yevgeny Prigozhin, head of the Wagner Mercenaries – led a 36-hr armed insurrection in June 2023. He captured the southern Russian city of Rostov-on-Don and sent his men to within 200 km of Moscow before retreating to Belarus and was then later assassinated.

We don't know what will happen going forward, but we do know that Ukrainians, well supported and supplied with the tools and arms needed will continue to fight for their country and their freedom. We need to continue supporting them however we can ensure that result.

Master the power of proactive training – Invite Bob to work with your teams

Regaining your freedom (time) means passing along some of those non-vital things to others by effective delegation. Right now, I bet you can think of at least three activities you hate that you haven't 'had time' to train someone else to do. Right?

Make the time! Until you do, you will never be free. Invest a day now to train and hand off at least one of these items. This will save you un-countless hours as you move forward and allow you to focus on your 'vital few' activities that actually move you forward. Effective leaders create time to train and delegate. This frees them up and it also lays a foundation for emerging leaders to grow!

Qualities of an EFFECTIVE leader, trainer, or coach

The author pictured here with Elisabeth Grimaud, AFCP (French Speakers Association) following his opening keynote in Paris, France August 2015 *Photo by Frédéric Bélot*

Becoming a more effective leader, trainer, or coach means learning to draw on and add to your abilities and skills to lead, equip, train, and motivate those who need your help. I've learned the importance of these qualities and have been diligently working to enhance them in my own efforts. They work in management situations, on the job, and in the leadership, co-ordination, and management of volunteers as well.

They are *solid* people skills, which will serve you well as you seek to take on larger leadership roles. They will help as you seek to assist, equip, and motivate those you lead to succeed in theirs.

Here are some of the traits of the more successful and effective leaders, trainers, and coaches I've worked with over the years.

Good communications skills

- Use clear, concise language to instruct, direct, and coach
- Make sure they not only *hear* you, but *understand* what you say
- Use active listening skills to draw them out and fully understand them
- Maintain eye contact

Solid understanding of the subject

- Comprehensive understanding of the subject or skills necessary to succeed
- Willingness to draw from your background as a bridge or foundation to teach or reach your team
- Willingness to grow and update your professional development

Experience

- It helps if you have done the job personally *Doing it well would be good, too!* ☺
- Previous experience in leadership or training helps
- Work to expand your experience and expertise. On the grow!

Patience

- New people can make mistakes while they learn – be patient
- It often takes a few tries to get it right (*keep up the encouragement*)
- Remember how it was *for you* when you first started out?

Interest in being an effective trainer and coach

- You need to *truly* enjoy helping people succeed
- Seeing people grow and learn makes you feel good
- Seeing others succeed gives you a sense of pride and satisfaction
- Leaders (*real leaders*) gain their greatest satisfaction from seeing their team grow and win in their changing roles

Genuine respect for other people

- People view you as being knowledgeable (*you model it*)
- People view you as being trustful and trustworthy (*you've earned it by your actions and your example*)
- People see you as being respectful and supportive (*you show it*)

Well-developed sense of humour

- You see the humour in the situation (*you express it*)
- You don't take yourself or life too seriously (*you lighten it*)
- Humour will help with the rough spots and bumps that happen

Having or acquiring these qualities and skills won't *guarantee* your success as a leader, trainer, or coach. They will, however, give you a better opportunity to do your job effectively. If you are seriously committed to building your career and want to expand into leadership or management, or are already a leader, then these qualities need to be an active part of how you live your life in that role.

The more you demonstrate these qualities and activities, the more your team will respond to your leadership, and the more productive they will become.

When they respond, they win, and so do you!

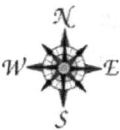

"Management is about persuading people to do things they do not want to do, while leadership is about inspiring people to do things, they never thought they could."   **Steve Jobs**

Peter Kossowan, PDD, DTM
Leaving a true legacy of leadership

My friend **Peter Kossowan, DTM, PDG** was featured on the cover with a story in the June 2016 issue of the **Toastmasters Magazine** for his amazing contribution to the lives of countless thousands of fellow Toastmasters, including myself.

At the time of the article, he had helped charter 164 clubs and shared some tips to follow in our own efforts. (**Update 2024:** Now over 172 clubs and at 93 he is still active in 3 of them as well as continuing to help others get going.) **Inspirational.**

Picture courtesy Greg Gazin, DTM, PDG Taken on the presentation of the Queen Elizabeth II Platinum Jubilee Medal to mark the 70the anniversary of her accession in 1952. Outstanding volunteers who made a positive impact of society were deemed eligible to receive the medals. We were proud of Peter's well-deserved recognition.

I first met Peter when I moved to Alberta in the fall of 2000. I visited Wild Rose and immediately joined. Peter and I are still active in Wild Rose Advanced Toastmasters as well as the D99 Past District Governor/District Director council. He is a positive encourager and at 93, still extremely active as a leader and shining example of what a Toastmaster can be.

We call him **"Mr. Toast!"** I am privileged to call him my friend! We've traded advice, stories, speeches, and evaluations over the years. He has helped me both as a speaker, friend, and a leader!

We are fortunate to have former Toastmasters leaders in our Wild Rose Advanced Club who continue to serve and encourage us. People like my friend **Neil Wilkinson**, DTM, Past International President *(recently honored for 50-yrs in leadership)*, **Ken Tanner**, DTM and **Carol Blair**, DTM, both Past International Directors. Leaders who freely give of themselves and lead a legacy of inspiration and encouragement.

Peter's remarkable 53-year plus Toastmaster journey launched in 1970 and is a testament to his passion about community service and his commitment to our members. Over the years, he served in leadership roles in dozens of community groups in the greater Edmonton area, earning the respect of fellow leaders around the province. He is a wise man with a welcoming smile and a wealth of experience and connections to share. We are privileged to have him in our club.

As he said, He was invited to visit a Toastmasters club and saw the value in what Toastmasters could bring to improving his financial planning business by enhancing his listening skills and presentations.

Along the way he increased his sales-closing techniques… skills he certainly used to help charter the 172 clubs over the years. Wow, and I thought 15 was a lot. If you are ever a visitor in a Toastmasters Club and Peter is there, don't be surprised if he invites you to join. ☺

When I decided to expand **Legacy of Leadership,** I thought, "What a great opportunity to say thanks to my friend Peter who has been a shinning example of leadership and service for so many of us in Toastmasters." Thanks Peter!

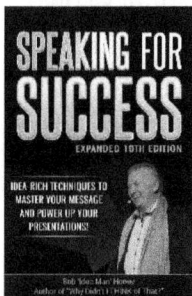

As a leader, I have found the ability to capture and arrange my thoughts helpful in coveying my ideas and building working relationships. One of the best places to hone your skills is **www.Toastmasters.org** Visit the website to find a club near you.

Visit **www.SuccessPublications.ca** to get your copy of **Speaking for Success** Expanded 10th edition

Observing and measuring performance
Idea-rich keys to effective leadership and coaching

If you are dedicated to helping those you lead or supervise improve in their performance and productivity, it helps to watch them in action. Ever notice how a *professional coach* in the athletic arena uses on-site observation and video replays? **This allows them to isolate and work on the specific areas, techniques, or skills needing work.**

In the business world, these *instant replays* can be filtered or edited by the people reporting them to the coach/manager. It is difficult to know how well someone is doing without observing or tracking their performance. Developing focused systems and garnering strategic information can lead to a better results and more effective coaching which leads to more effective performance.

Over the years, one of my leadership challenges was to work closely with those I supervised, to train them to be more productive on the job. I've had a fair amount of challenge as a small business owner, additionally as a manager for larger firms, in helping my employees succeed.

Long before coaching became a 'buzz' word, I found myself using some of these leadership success techniques in coaching my staff, helping set goals for learning, and honing their skill sets so they could enhance their ability to be promoted.

Back in the mid 70's, I was hired to open a Big Boy's franchise in Edmonton Center. A year or so later, I was asked to go to Calgary and assist the franchiser owner there in re-energizing his staff. After my departure, my two assistant managers were promoted, one to take over my store and the second one to take over a store in the east side of the city. Their skills had been honed and they then had the chance to shine.

In the 90's, I had a similar opportunity when I was head-hunted as part of the management team to open the first two Home Depots in BC. Several of my staff were later tapped to move up into management as additional stores were opened. Several went on to successfully lead and manage other firms.

Coaching, as part of the training and motivational process, works very well. It works well in the association market in leading volunteers, too. There are several success stories of boards and those who serve on them who responded well to coaching techniques.

One example was during my extended term as President of CAPS-Vancouver, BC (1999 and 2000). We had a challenge in that we had an almost zero bank balance, low membership, and low energy in our meetings. We also had a reluctant president (me) who took office 10 months earlier than he had expected. ☺

It took recruiting a motivated team, one-by-one, to make it happen and to reverse the process. It took a coach/leader to call the plays, help set the goals, and continue helping our volunteer leaders grow to take on their respective roles and to serve the membership. Did it work? You bet it did!

At the end of our term, we had tripled our membership; had a healthy bank account; a reasonable budget for the next year; solid guidelines and procedures; a 2-year succession of leaders (both succeeding presidents did awesome jobs); a healthy, fully active board; the next year's meetings and guest speakers booked; and a very relieved Immediate Past President. ☺

Our national association recognized our growth in 2000 by awarding us CAPS Chapter of the Year. Our National President, Pat Katz, CSP, HoF awarded me a special CAPS President's Award "...for my energetic contribution to the advancement of CAPS and my living example of the power of one."

Yes, coaching as a leadership skill works, well!

Successful managers (leaders and coaches) **look at both the results and the process** to find areas where they can assist their employees to fine tune, hone, add to, or tweak their skills for enhanced performance and productivity. They use coaching as one of their strategic tools to assist their teams to succeed.

Performance observation and measurements must be done on a regular, recurring basis to offer ongoing *validity* in your coaching efforts. I have found that a little personal feedback and instruction *closer to the activity* is the most effective. Performance reviews, as done in most businesses once or twice a year, are not effective and can at times be counterproductive.

Learning how to observe your employees without making them feel intimidated or uncomfortable is a skill you'll need to acquire as you evolve your coaching expertise.

- **What do you see?**
- **What did they do?**
- **What worked well?**
- **What can be improved?**
- **What needs clarification?**
- **What needs additional explanation or training?**
- **What needs to be changed in the way they are asked to do things?**
- **What can they teach you?**

Helping your employees and volunteers grow will require work on your part to observe their performance, design systems to help measure their performance, and allow you to give them the positive, helpful feedback they need.

It can be hard work! But your investment in their growth will pay dividends in the future, dividends in increased performance, improved morale and team building, and enhanced productivity.

"If your actions create a legacy that inspires others to dream more, learn more, do more and become more, then, you are an excellent leader."

Dolly Parton

I've included Leadership videos as a bonus for our Legacy of Leadership readers. Simply follow this link to access: *https://www.youtube.com/user/ideamanbob*

How to avoid 'expensive' training mistakes

As a **leading-edge owner, executive, manager, or team leader** you may be asked to make decisions to engage or contract on programs and policies that will either help or hinder your team in reaching their goals. You can avoid making *major, career limiting, expensive,* training mistakes by considering a few ideas and side-stepping some of these mistakes that have minimized returns on training dollars.

Unfortunately training dollars are ultimately *wasted* when leaders make some or all the following mistakes.

- **Failing to fully assess team needs**

Perhaps you are teaching your team skills they already have? Team members don't need training 'just for the sake of training'. I've heard managers say, ***"Even if they know this stuff– a refresher won't hurt them!"***

Sometimes that is true (*I have been asked back to reinforce a program or to provide add-on sessions or coaching*). If not handled correctly, it can be counter-productive to your end goals or de-motivating to your team.

Here's an idea-rich suggestion

Before you launch any training program, conduct a needs assessment with your team. Work to establish a *comprehensive list of skills* of current team members. This way you may discover what they already know and what they need (and hopefully want) to learn. Then, as you provide training, it will send a positive message that reinforces the idea that you value their contributions and are dedicated to helping them increase and hone their skills.

Decide to strategically design your training programs to incorporate follow up reinforcement to enhance their effectiveness. Make that a vital part of your program and design it to ensure it is productive reinforcement not a perceived punishment.

- **Thinking (wishfully) that training sessions will eliminate conflict**

Leaders and managers sometimes think that training, especially training that focuses on team or relationship building, will eliminate conflict on the job. Some programs over emphasize teamwork at the expense of **team-effectiveness.**

All team efforts need to be focused, task and relationship oriented. When sessions focus *too much* on relationship building vs. team-effectiveness they lose impact and may become counter-productive.

Team building is a very important aspect of any successful business or organization. Make sure it is not *sacrificed* in replacement for **team-effectiveness.** Professional leadership is being able to work with people who may 'bug you' and being able to direct their efforts to help the team succeed.

Here's an idea-rich suggestion

Work diligently to ensure everyone on your team understands that *constructive* conflict is an important part of the team process. Without some conflict and honest difference of opinion, you get mediocrity. As someone once told me, ***"The opposite of conflict is apathy, not peace and harmony."***

The secret is in not taking conflict as a *personal issue* or a negative result in the process. Creative, constructive conflict can be a *strategic* part of a positive process in making sure your team makes the right choice and (time permitting) fully explores all the options and potential pitfalls.

- **Thinking of training as a program vs. a process**

One of the challenges in training is the expectation that a half-day, full day or even a few days of training can change years of embedded habit.

Research shows that shorter sessions, with reinforced follow-up, spread over a longer time result in better retention and long-range effectiveness. *Short and often* rather than a one-time massive attack seems to work better. That is one of the reasons behind the success of our spaced online video training programs.

Here's an idea-rich suggestion

For your training to be effective, insights and ideas gained during programs must be quickly translated into action (**Ideas At Work!**) – actions that are reinforced by the leaders on your team. Real development is never completed, as is the true essence of education.

In our live sessions, audience members are challenged to make a special commitment to act on what they learn and to schedule those actions.

Visit: www.ideaman.net for more information.

I hope these suggestions will help you as you search out the most effective training programs for your team. I'd be happy to share some other thoughts with you if you have any other questions or queries. Of course, I would be happy to explore how I might be of service in on-site training for you and your team. Send me a note at: **bob@ideaman.net**

I shared these points at the 12th annual HR Summit in Manila in 2019.

"Be a yardstick of quality. Some people aren't used to an environment where excellence is expected."
Steve Jobs

Source point
A leader's guide to power and how to focus it for best results

A power failure can have disastrous results in people's lives. Whole communities can be affected. Vital facilities, such as hospitals, maintain back-up generators for such an eventuality. Their equipment must function – lives depend on it.

I live in the country, in a little hamlet, in the northeast part of Alberta. It is peaceful and quiet and somewhat secluded. It is my creative place. Occasionally we experience power outages. Thankfully they have not been extended; but I prepared for just such an occurrence. Simple logic and thinking ahead, really.

Power and the means to apply it are critical to our industrialized, increasingly knowledge based, e-influenced society. Energy costs escalate and sometimes energy sources dry up. People conserve energy and cut back. Once again, (like the 1980's) we see fleets of large jets mothballed because of the high price of aviation fuel. 2005 saw oil prices skyrocket to record highs and the price at the pump and airfares went crazy. 2008-2012 saw similar rises and economic challenges. Recently, we've seen oil drop dramatically. Just as bad!

The 2003 blackout in eastern parts of the country brought home our dependence on power to many people. We've had many more since then. Our daily lives depend, in various degrees, on a readily available power source. We need electricity to power our machines, light our paths, and allow us to communicate with each other and the world. We need fuel for our vehicles and to heat our houses.

So too, do **we as leaders, depend on a power source**, as we continue to tackle the challenges we've taken on. Each of us has a leadership role. Our lives have the power to impact and radically transform the future.

We must have clear access to that *source point* of power if we are to truly impact the world around us and fulfill our vision and purpose. We already have power *resident* in our daily lives if we *just* source it:

- **Power to dream**
- **Power to create**
- **Power to choose**
- **Power to change**
- **Power to lead**

Our energy level does not question the need but responds to our mental conditioning and inner motivation. Have you ever found yourself mentally fatigued, exhausted, and without energy? Then, someone asks you to do something you really enjoy or are totally committed to doing. What happens? Instantaneously, you shrug off your fatigue and excitedly rise to the new challenge, the new opportunity. Why is that? Where did the energy or *power* come from?

What then is our *source point* as leaders and how do we access it at will?

In studies of powerful leaders throughout history, leaders with vision who inspired me to action, I've noticed two shared traits. Shared areas in how they lived their lives and how they contributed to the world; shared areas that act as a *source point*.

- A deep conviction in a purpose greater than themselves
- Harnessed belief in their own God given abilities and skills

As leaders, we must continually guard our *source point* against all the demands and frustrations crying for our attention that would drain our energy.

"Business more than any other occupation is a continual dealing with the future; it is a continual calculation, and instinctive exercise in foresight."
Henry R. Luce

Here are some tips that have been very helpful to me in that quest over the past 29 plus years

Dream big – commit big!

Small dreams have no power to inspire you or those who would follow you to act. Big dreams help focus big purpose and big purpose promotes self-esteem and dignity. **Make time to dream!** Then commit to acting NOW on that dream!

I remember sitting across the table from my new friend, mentor, and fellow speaker, business expert and leader **Peter J. Daniels**. *I remember having him challenge me on my dreams when I was first starting down this path of professional leadership, speaking, and training. We were sitting in a little fish and chips place in downtown Adelaide, Australia and he told me '...my dreams were too small'. I was shocked! It must have shown on my face.* ☺ *He then went on to challenge me to raise my sights and make my dreams big enough to inspire me and those who would seek to help me along the path during the tough times. He was so right!*

My thanks to Peter as well as my amazing friends throughout the **Global Speakers Federation** who have been instrumental in my growth and ongoing success as a leader and in my commitment to my clients and audiences.

Focus your energy

Clear, concise, concrete goals help focus and direct your energy to fulfilling your ultimate, most significant purpose. Guard against diluting your focus or diluting your power by over-committing yourself and spreading yourself too thin. **Make time to refine and refocus your goals.** Use your goals as a filter to make decisions on the investment of your time and energy.

Ask yourself,

- *"Is this activity, itself, important?"*
- *"Is this activity important for 'ME' to be involved in?"*

One of my biggest challenges, in a variety of professional and volunteer leadership roles, was in learning how to be wiser in committing time. I am learning to say '**NO'** more often. I am an *'idea man'* as well as a *hands-on-let's-see-how-we-can-make-this-work* kind of guy. That's why I call my company **Ideas At Work! – Strategies for Success!** This would seem to be a good thing, right?

Not always so in leadership. *The lesson learned, painfully at times, was to allow others to take personal leadership on their ideas and for me to act as their cheerleader, coach, and champion of their success.*

The result – *we each achieved more than if I had tried to play an active part in the implementation of an intriguing idea. The other result – people who might not have had the opportunity stood up and took personal leadership. They did a better job because it was their decision and commitment to make it happen. They took the lead!*

People will often rise to a challenge if we allow them the opportunity. Expect the best, challenge them, coach them, and then cheer them on to success!

I saw it at work in Toastmasters, as BC's District 21 Governor; in my challenge as President to rebuild our CAPS-BC chapter; on our CAPS National Board; on our CAPS Foundation Board; and in a host of other organizations where I had a chance to share my ideas in a leadership role. Hmmm – a double win!

Commit yourself

Commit yourself to achieving your ultimate purpose, fulfilling your dream, and reaching your goals in pursuit of worthy endeavours. Committing your life to something worthwhile will give you the motivation and energy you need to get the job done and not burn yourself out doing it. **Make the time to commit and commit wisely!**

"Commitment is the enemy of resistance for it is the serious promise to press on, to get up, no matter how many times you have been knocked down."
David McNally

Commitment is an interesting thing. So easily given and so difficult to sustain. All too easily, sidetracked and put aside.

Commitments *kept* are the foundation of our true success in life and in providing effective and powerful leadership that makes a difference in the lives of those we lead, and in our careers and communities.

- What empowers **you** as a leader?
- What moves **you** to follow through on your commitments?
- What makes **you** get up in the morning ready to tackle the world?
- What helps **you** maintain your energy?
- What makes **you** dig deep into your reserves and then even further to make something you've committed to happen or to keep your word or commitment?

"There is only one way to succeed in anything and that is to give it everything. I do and I demand that my players do. Any man's finest hour is when he has worked his heart out in a good cause and lies exhausted on the field of battle... victorious."

Vince Lombardi

These questions and your *honest* answers will help you determine your personal *source point*.

Guard it, care for it, feed it with positive action and personal motivation so that it grows and becomes even more evident in your life. It will make a difference in the quality of your life and in the results of your leadership of those who entrust you with their future.

"The leaders who work most effectively, it seems to me, never say 'I'. And that's not because they have trained themselves not to say 'I'. They don't think 'I'. They think 'we'; they think 'team'. They understand their job to be to make the team function. They accept responsibility and don't sidestep it, but 'we' gets the credit. This is what creates trust, what enables you to get the task done."

Peter Drucker

Change is a creative choice

"Searching for the peak performer within yourself has one basic meaning - You recognize yourself as a person who was born, not as a peak performer, but as a learner. With the capacity to grow, change, and reach for the highest possibilities of human nature, you regard yourself as a person in process. Not perfect, but a person who keeps asking: What more can I be? What else can I achieve that will benefit me and my company? That will contribute to my family and my community?"

Charles Garfield

In life and leadership, we frequently have the opportunity *thrust upon us* to make changes. A death, a major illness, **or a major economic upheaval** can force us to take stock of our lives at that point and sometimes make radical changes. The attack on 9-11 did that for many of us. So did Covid-19 on a global basis. It sure did for me.

In our changing economy, we find many businesses and professional associations being stretched and tested as competition and demand for service become global. Leadership and staffing have become more challenging and so has training and marketing. Clients are becoming more demanding and specific in what they want.

Applied creativity is an under-utilized leadership skill. The most productive leaders are often the most creative in their dealings with teams. Change is pushed on us everywhere we turn. We can't avoid change, can we? Avoiding change is what too many business leaders think about and accordingly they miss their full potential. They miss the opportunity to rethink how they see and deal with change in their lives and their businesses.

Wouldn't it be better to *seize the opportunities* to change and grow? Isn't it more effective to be a leader who is open to learn, stretch, and push yourself past your comfort zone?

Change is a creative choice! Life is a series of changes and choices, why not control their direction and pace?

Ask yourself a few questions. Allow your *honest* reactions to reflect the changes in your attitudes and actions that may need to be addressed to maximize your life and business dealings. Your answers can form a guide for your leadership path and growth.

- What do I really want my life to accomplish? What is the biggest dream or goal for my life?
- What would I like my company/team to accomplish?
- Where do I want my leadership and career to go?
- Where would I like to see my team change, grow, and succeed?
- What am I afraid of? What is stopping me? What keeps me up at night?
- What do I need to change to make it work? When do I need to change it?
- When will I commit to start making these changes?

Will you have the courage to change? Will you commit to your best and to creatively building your business or association to leverage and maximize its potential? Remember the words of wisdom from pioneer retailer **J.C. Penny**, *"No one need live a minute longer as he/she is, because the creator endowed us with the ability to change ourselves."*

Answering these questions will have given you a *glimpse* of what needs to be changed to make your leadership dreams and goals a reality. The secret is in putting foundations under your dreams and actions to your goals. The leadership secret to fully **unlocking your 'creative' potential** is in accessing your ability to embrace and use change for mutual benefit. **The choice is yours!**

"If you want to teach people a new way of thinking, don't bother trying to teach them. Instead, give them a tool, the use of which will lead to new ways of thinking."

Buckminster Fuller

Innovate or evaporate – the time to act is NOW!

When would be the best time to begin some serious leadership involvement and work on nurturing a culture of innovation in your organization? **Now!** is the short answer.

They say, *"The best time to plant bamboo is 20 years ago. The second-best time to plant is now!"* The *actual* or *virtual* gap between imagination and achievement or actualization has never been shorter. **Act now!**

Beginning *somewhere* is always preferable to waiting while your team or upper management weighs *all* the options, or while the organization goes bust or gets left in the dust by those competitors who *are* being innovative and creative in this volatile market.

Author of **'Leading the Revolution'**, **Gary Hamel** advocates that *"...radical innovation is the competitive advantage of the new millennium."* With the aftermath of 9-11, the Enron fallout, and a general shake up in our economy following 2008, a major wakeup call is *still* very much in order. Our current challenges – still do!

J.K. Galbraith, noted economist, once shared, *"Faced with the choice of changing one's mind and proving there is no need to – almost everyone gets busy on the proof."* But that process can be a leadership challenge to productive change with some organizations' mental constraints and *'stuck-in-the-mud'* mindsets.

Everyone needs to be involved. *Partial* commitment to innovation is commitment to failure. There needs to be a *demonstrated* willingness to listen to and act on the plan for change that comes from this consultative innovation process.

Creative Partners' Andy Radka shared the results of a survey of 500 top North American CEO's.

They were asked what their organization needed to survive in the 21st Century.

- Their top answer was "…to practice creativity and innovation."
- However, only 6% of them believed they were tackling this effectively.

Quite a gap between expressed needs and application. Obviously, blending in a ***spirit of innovation*** takes time vs. a quick fix or special workshop or seminar (*even idea-rich ones like mine* ☺).

If innovation and creativity are *so important,* even critical in business survival; why is there such a gap in application and implementation? Innovation in organizational structure and action is very crucial.

While each organization is distinct and different, there needs to be a more holistic, integrated approach to innovation and creativity as a culture. We need to get *buy-in* on all levels. Further, we need to consider some important points to increase the possibility of idea generation, which in turn, drive innovation and creativity in any organization.

What can you do to facilitate this process? Here are some areas of concern or consideration in building a foundation for success under this creative and innovative initiative.

Innovation strategy

Innovation needs to be an *integral part* of all strategies and policies in your organization, not just *tacked* on as a quick fix up. It needs to permeate every department and every section of your organization. Every employee must be encouraged to make it part of their focus as they conduct their respective roles.

For example, how much time is spent in the boardroom or around a planning table discussing ongoing innovation strategy? This is where the *rubber hits the road,* and your employees/volunteers/clients see just how much you are committed to this path of action.

Support from top management

In too many organizations, ideas and innovative steps are *already at risk* at their inception. Senior leadership can look the other way **or** take the courageous step and stretch out a helping hand to buoy them until they can be worked out, be tested, and tried in the real world.

Ask yourself, "Do my fellow managers see themselves as leaders whose role is to **'clear the way' for creativity** or are they simply status quo oriented?" Your employees and colleagues are watching for your leadership in this arena. What will your employees and colleagues see when they observe your leadership in action?

Collective mindsets

Whether we acknowledge it or not, we *each* have mindsets comprised of beliefs, attitudes, and values that drive or motivate our behaviour. These collective mindsets (e.g., *"can't teach old dog's new tricks"* or *"my people aren't creative"*) frequently form barriers to the creative process.

They need to be unlocked, unblocked, and unleashed!

Business guru **Peter Drucker** once said, *"...defending yesterday – i.e., not innovating – is far riskier than making tomorrow."*

Make sure your organizational *mindset* is not creating an *immune system* or *anti-viral system* that automatically rejects or attacks new ideas, processes, or challenges to the *status quo* business model. This can be your largest obstacle in *embedding* creative approaches and applied innovation throughout your organization.

Employees get tools and training

Are your staff /volunteers being given the right tools and the on-going training they need to support a creative and innovative climate? **People and strategic training are crucial to your success** and the training needs to be ongoing and reinforced. Creativity will not *magically* flourish with the advent of a few courses or the provision of a *few* creative tools to a *few select* people.

Each person needs to be trained and supported in his or her evolution of understanding and applied learning. This is *true* leadership.

Knowledge management tools

Does your organization have an intranet that leverages or capitalizes on the advancement information technology has brought to the battle for business growth, expansion, or survival?

I.T. (Information Technology) often acts as an enabler, allowing us to break the traditional barriers of function, geography, and even hierarchy. *It can help bring down repressive political regimes too.* This allows for internet-based sparking of ideas and a chance to engage and bring 'all' the minds of your various teams into the game. This is how you win!

For example: A few years back, Titleist asked permission to use 5 of my articles on a new intranet site they set up for their sales staff across North America. Of course, I was pleased to say yes.

What gets measured gets done – metrics for innovation

Creativity and innovation can be measured and, if so, are done on a more consistent basis. If creativity is rewarded, even more! Intellectual assets can impact heavily on your market value. Consider the differential costs between hardware and software values.

Creation of an 'idea-rich' pipeline

Is there an effective innovation process, pipeline, or some form of tracking system for capturing and converting ideas into innovative services or new products?

Is everyone on your team committed to feeding this process or pipeline? Just as in the sales process, you need to feed your pipeline to have solid, sustainable business opportunities. Only solid systematic processes, which incorporate a blend of logical and lateral thinking tools, can bring creativity and innovation.

What are you doing to ensure you *prime the pump* and keep this innovation pipeline full and the leadership and business building ideas flowing?

Supplier and client mindsets

Organizations create a demand for innovative suppliers to be able to better serve their clients who are more often demanding innovative products and services.

Ask yourself, *"Are your current (and potential) clients able to support a dialogue about inventing your shared future?"* How about your suppliers and allied professionals? They may not even recognize the future, until they see it or are made aware of its possibilities. That, in part, is your job, the connection and education process of business.

Just a few thoughts to consider in your quest for increased creativity and applied innovation at the company or organization you lead. **The time to act is now!** Innovate or evaporate in the dust of those competitors who saw the need, made the investment, and took the lead. *It's your choice!*

First ladies of leadership

I met Helen at an NSA convention as she was working on her book. We got to know each other better at a Toastmasters International convention where we both presented. I loved this lady of leadership's spirit.

Helen Blanchard, DTM, PIP, **Author of Breaking the Ice** *(1926-2013) and avid Toastmaster - Int'l President 1985-86 (honoured to be the first woman to serve in that position). When she needed help in her professional pursuits, Helen joined Toastmasters International, then a male-only organization. Forced to join under the assumed name, "Homer," she ultimately rose to lead this organization as its first female president. Hers is a story of hard work, dedication, guts, smarts, and friendship. Helen won the hearts of acquaintances, supervisors, co-workers — and most of all — her fellow members of Toastmasters International. She paved the way for women to join Toastmasters, to participate fully, and to dare to dream of leadership roles. Sadly, we lost this leader in 2013 and many of us remember her with gratitude.*

Leadership skills are changing; are yours?

- **Leadership** and working with teams can be fun. It can also be an exercise in futility and frustration, if done ineffectively.
- **Leading** is an acquired skill in the art of working with people, helping them focus their efforts on a common goal or team objective.

If you seek to be an *effective 21st century leader*, a reflective look at this list of leadership styles, activities, or attributes might be in order. Ask yourself how many of these you exhibit as you seek to lead those men and women who have entrusted you with their concerns and trust.

What needs to change for you to become more effective in your leadership? Perhaps being more...

Responsible

Do you take full responsibility for your actions and decisions? Do you also take responsibility for their end results? Are you responsible, accountable, and available when decisions are made, and steps taken by your team? True leaders take 100% responsibility for their lives.

Growth focused

Are you an *on-the-grow* leader, who is committed to seeking out new ideas, new methods, and new alliances to help serve those you lead? Are you a leader who is also a reader, seeking knowledge to help you lead?

Exemplary

Do you walk your talk? Do your motives, actions, and attitudes reflect the person, the leader, you would honestly like to become?

Inspiring

Do you inspire confidence and trust in those who follow you? Can you call them to action, in solving your mutual challenges?

Efficient

Do you use your time as well as the time of those you serve wisely? Do they see you using your time in productive activities on their behalf? Do you have time to fully do your job? Do you make time to LEAD?

Caring

Do your people know from *first-hand* experience that you care about them? Do you model it as you move through your day?

Communicating

How are you at sharing your ideas, listening to the needs and concerns of your people, and making sure that you fully understand them? Do you make sure they are well informed about what the challenges and your proposed solutions to those changes entail?

Competent

This strikes at the heart of your ability to deliver the goods for your people. Are you competent to do the job and do it well?

Goal oriented

Are you a leader who is effective in setting realistic goals, communicating those goals, and gathering people to support the attainment of those common goals? Are you a leader who achieves the worthwhile goals set for the common good?

Decisive

Can you make an *informed* decision and *act* on that decision quickly? Or do you study a challenge to death and continually put off making a decision while waiting for more information?

Unifying

Are you a leader who seeks to *include* everyone involved and works hard to make sure no one is excluded? Are you a leader who builds bonds between diverse groups with conflicting agendas and viewpoints? Are you a leader who can earn their trust and allow them to get past their divisiveness and get behind you in accomplishing something in everyone's best interest? Are you a creative catalyst for commitment and concrete action?

Working

Are you a leader who is committed to working on behalf of those who trust you? A leader who is not afraid to get their hands dirty, dig in, and lead by example; to do what is needed to get the job done successfully? Are you a leader who sets an *energetic pace* and is fully engaged working out the solutions and to engaging people in the partnership of performance in achieving common goals?

Tough list, isn't it? Yes, it is!

If you would truly seek to be a 21st century leader these are the skills that will assist you in successfully serving and leading your people.

Are you willing to take charge and lead change?

"The challenge of leadership is to be strong, but not rude; be kind, but not weak; be bold, but not bully; be thoughtful, but not lazy; be humble, but not timid; be proud, but not arrogant; have humor, but without folly."

Jim Rohn

Maxwell on leadership... a few thoughts

"Leadership is a lifestyle of commitment, not a label.
If people willingly follow you – you are a leader. If not, you simply have a label."
Bob 'Idea Man' Hooey

Over the last couple of decades, I have learned more than a few idea-rich *lessons on leadership.* ☺ Many lessons came the hard way by making mistakes and by taking some un-seen detours and encountering dead ends. Some gleaned through the successful achievement of teams I had the privilege of leading and/or learning along-side.

More recently, (*over the past 20 plus years*) I have been accepting more opportunities for sharing my ideas and lessons learned from my personal leadership journey. I have been devouring the thoughts and ideas of other leadership speakers and writers to *fill out* and add to my *understanding* of this essential but elusive success skill.

"People buy into a leader first, then the vision."
John C. Maxwell

You may have heard the name John C. Maxwell. He is an expert on the subject of leadership, having written about it in 30 plus books and spoken to millions around the world. His *'The 21 Irrefutable Laws of Leadership',* was a business best seller. A leader who talks his walk!

John addressed an audience of Toastmaster leaders awhile back. He shared *solid* ideas with us on the building blocks of a successful personality and their importance to us as leaders. I took lots of notes.

He talked about:
- The ability to get along with others (*relationship building*),
- The ability to share our vision (*equipping*), and
- A positive *attitude* and leadership ability.

John went on to stress that although all of these traits are important, *"everything rises and falls on leadership"*. If you want to be effective in your career or business, hone your leadership skills. According to John, leadership ability is the *lid* that determines your effectiveness.

(Irrefutable law #1) Leadership skills are not honed or built overnight. According to Maxwell, **"They are developed daily by reading, listening, attending workshops and conferences, and sharing ideas."** (*Made sense to me.*☺)

"Successful leaders are learners." The learning process is ongoing, a result of self-discipline and perseverance. Our goal each day must be to get better, to build on the previous day's progress! *Worth repeating.*

According to Maxwell, *"All great leaders share the ability to build and lead teams."* He went on to challenge us with these statements.

- *"One is too small a number to achieve greatness."* Building a team is difficult, but you cannot do anything significant without one. A group is not a team.
- *"A team shares a vision, mindset, and heart."* The compounding of great ideas happens in a team. A great idea is the result of several good ideas.
- *"A team is not a team without a leader they can trust and follow!"* Leadership functions on trust. Trust is the foundation upon which every relationship – at work, at home, in the community, or anywhere else – is built.

Trust is earned and according to Maxwell, you only receive it when you have these **three key attributes: character, competence, and consistency.** When these attributes mesh, you begin to build and receive trust from others.

A closer look at these three key attributes reveals or underscores the fact they are built or developed over time. Leadership is a *'process of progress'* towards increased trust and responsibility.

Bob: my personal experience: *"Leadership is a choice, not a label."* You keep earning trust as you keep learning. Trust is a fragile thing and, once lost, very difficult to recover or rebuild.

Leadership is a lifestyle of commitment to increased service and guidance of those you have under your care. Warren Bennis says, *"Without trust, the leader cannot function."*

John went on to share these ***strategic steps*** he felt would help keep us on track in our leadership journey and keep us from eroding or losing the trust of our team. Here are my reflections on those steps he shared.

Focus on shared goals more than personal agendas

When it comes to trust, it is not about you. You are leading the company, office, or team for the benefit of everyone. People will not follow you if it becomes apparent that you are just in it for yourself. What is in it for them? Remember **"You win when they win!"**

Stay away from petty or divisive politics

Make sure everyone knows you cannot be bought or compromised. Keep this a clear and *visible* focus. The quickest way to derail or destroy your leadership is to get entangled in factions or frictions. Leadership integrity is empowering, not entangling.

Do the right thing regardless of personal risk

Being a leader means sometimes you must grit your teeth and take the pain when doing the right thing causes you to get hurt. That is the essence of leadership – choosing to do what is right regardless of the cost. This can be your biggest challenge and test. Those whom you seek to lead will be watching and judging your ability to lead by *how* you act and what you choose. Choose wisely!

Be fully accountable to others

Perhaps you can create an *unofficial* advisory board of trusted colleagues, coaches, or mentors to keep tabs on how you're doing in these steps.

Don't rely on your own judgement as the only way to keep you on track. **The wisdom of many can be a guide to the leader.** *I have several trusted advisors, as well as a success team, who help keep me focused and on track. I value their insights, honesty, and input tremendously.*

Follow the Golden Rule

Treat people the way you want to be treated. It's simple and it still works after all these years, even more so for leaders and aspiring leaders. This is so simple and yet so difficult for many who would seek to lead. ***"You lead by example, if you would lead at all!"***

Make sure what you say matches what you do

Consistency and *congruity* working in tandem underscore and demonstrate your credibility and competence. The best way to earn and maintain the trust of your team is to ***'Say what you mean and mean what you say'*** – and then model it! Lead by example works here!

When people see with their own eyes that you are trustworthy with both your words and your actions, they are more inclined to want to be a part of your team. This is the foundation for success in leadership!

Being a leader is not easy otherwise everyone would be doing it, effectively. Everyone who calls himself or herself a leader is not proven to be one in fact. Many who don't 'officially' take on the label; earn the respect and the position in people's minds and actions despite not choosing the limelight.

People will follow you when you demonstrate to them you are trustworthy of their commitment to you, and they buy into the vision you share. But remember John's sage advice, ***"People buy into the leader first, then the vision."***

Invest a few minutes to reflect on his **'three key leadership attributes: character, competence, and consistency'.**
Be totally honest with yourself. **How would you rate in each of these areas?**

- Would you see areas of improvement in your leadership skills?
- What would those you lead tell you about your rating in each of these key attributes?
- Perhaps chatting with your trusted colleagues and specifically asking them to give you their insight and feedback would be beneficial. Ask for their honest feedback – and heed it to grow in your leadership role.

Leadership is a lifelong journey.

Once you make the commitment, the path lies before you, beckoning you, teasing you, taunting you, testing you each step of the way. The journey can be challenging at times, after all you are dealing with people and the personalities that come with their involvement on your team.

The vision, the goal, the chance to make a difference is the *heart* that keeps your leadership blood pumping. **Enjoy the journey!**

First ladies of leadership

I include female leaders to encourage more women to step up and speak out. We need more qualified women in leadership roles.

Irene Gaudet *is my wife and an active partner in my various travel and adventures. She is a very smart (scientific role) and creative (web design), diligent woman. She also proofs my writing; on your behalf, for which I am very grateful!*

She is also a long-time (35 plus years) union activist who takes the lead in protecting the rights and safety of her fellow workers. She has earned respect throughout her involvements and in her various leadership roles in Alberta. She was inducted (2015) as a Life Member in AUPE. I have learned to appreciate her leadership in many of her roles, as have her colleagues.

A question of leadership?

Leadership is an important skill for anyone wanting to create or enhance a successful career. Leadership can lead to recognition and open doors to your success working for yourself or someone else.

Think about the following list of names for a moment.

Meg Whitman	Jack Welsh	Walt Disney
Mary Kay Ash	W. Clement Stone	Warren Buffet
Eiji Toyoda	YOU?	Sam Walton
Fred Smith	Lee Iacocca	Bill Gates
Michael Dell	Clive Beddoe	Steve Jobs

Ask yourself:

- What do they have in common?
- What do you know about them and/or their companies?
- What connections or commonalities do they share?

Now you might be thinking:

- Each of them started, built, or led a billion-dollar company employing thousands.
- Many of them started with very little capital, overcame struggles, and/or took on struggling organizations to re-create them and lead them to success.
- Each has gained national or international exposure and recognition for their leadership, success, and achievements.
- Each of them has become or was wealthy.
- Some have retired well or passed away.
- The majority are male; only two are women.

You would be correct. However, the connections I've drawn are slightly different. Let's take a minute to remind you of the organizations each of these leaders created or led to greater success.

- **Meg Whitman** started an on-line company called **eBay**
- **Mary Kay** Ash created the company that still bears her name
- **Eiji Toyoda** was part of the family who created **Toyota**
- **Fred Smith** launched **FedEx** which continues to deliver value
- **Michael Dell** started **Dell Computers** while still in college
- **Jack Welsh** was a legendary **GE** leader who created leaders and a very profitable, well-run company
- **W. Clement Stone** made his initial fortune in the insurance industry, but is best known for starting **Success Magazine** with **Napoleon Hill**; and hiring and mentoring one of my favourite motivational authors, **Og Mandino**
- **Lee Iacocca** took on the challenge of rebuilding **Chrysler** and saved them from bankruptcy
- **Clive Beddoe** was one of 4 founding partners with successful Calgary, AB based **WestJet**
- **Walt Disney** needs no introduction for his creative leadership
- **Warren Buffet** is still one of North America's savviest investors
- **Sam Walton** started a small store called **Wal-Mart** which grew to be the world's largest company
- **Bill Gates** created **Microsoft** and gave **Apple's Steve Jobs** someone to compete with ☺

Let me ask you two personal questions:
- Can you see *your* name included in the 'center' square at some time in your future? Yes? No? Why not?
- Do you see the *less obvious* connections?

Now you might be saying, "NO" to these questions. Some of you would say, *"No way, Bob! I can't see MY name included in this list of famous, influential, successful, and wealthy people."*

Why not?
What is stopping you from being included at some time in your future?

- Each of these took *personal leadership* over his/her life and business careers. Each created something of definite value for those who joined them in their quest.
- Each exhibited definite attributes of *true* leadership and effective management, which propelled them to succeed in their respective ventures.
- **Each spelled their *leadership* with multiple P's.** Their success and track record reinforce that observation. Each of them exhibited *all or most* of the following traits (P's) in various degrees of intensity in their life and their leadership. None of them started out rich or famous.

Each of us can learn from their example, build on their expertise, and expand our personal leadership success. Can you begin to see a glimpse of yourself here?

Look at the characteristics (below) observed in their successful leadership. Let me ask you again. *"Can you see yourself included?"* Perhaps you are now saying, *"Yes!"* That is great!

Each of you has the capacity to take personal leadership over your area and expand your leadership role. There is **not** one person reading this who has not exhibited some or all of these traits in various degrees or in specific situations. Wouldn't you agree? Ask your team?

Leaderships' multiple Ps:
- **Passion**
- **Purpose**
- **Principled**
- **Persistence**
- **Performance oriented**
- **Positive**
- **Perspective**
- **Persuasive**
- **People builders**
- **Pride of ownership**

Each of these traits can be honed and enhanced. Each of them is a learned and applied leadership success skill.

- What stops you from studying and working to enhance and expand your perspective and performance as a leader where you serve?
- What stops you from taking personal responsibility for your growth, involvement, and career success?
- What stops you from taking personal responsibility for your career and area of responsibility?

Only you! So why not go for it? Why not become that innovative leader? Are you willing to step up and take on that leadership role? Are you willing to be included in the list of people who continue to spell leadership with multiple P's?

It's really a question of leadership.

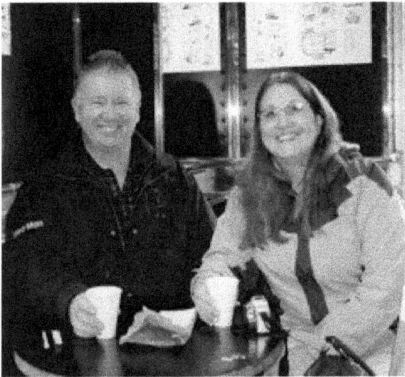

*My wife, Irene and I enjoying a coffee and croissants on the Eiffel tower. She met me in Paris on my way home from accepting an **'Excellence in Innovation Award'** while speaking in Mumbai, India. I'd suggested she meet me on my way home and celebrate her birthday week. She chose Paris.*

She is my active partner on my leadership journey. Thanks Irene.

 I've included some leadership videos for our readers. Simply follow this link to access them.
https://www.youtube.com/user/ideamanbob

Fortitude Vincimus
"By endurance we conquer!"

"Men wanted for Hazardous Journey. Small wages, bitter cold, long months of complete darkness, constant danger, and safe return doubtful. Honour and recognition in case of success."

I'm in, aren't you? ☺ This advertisement was placed in the London, England papers to recruit members of the British Imperial Trans-Antarctic expedition led by **Sir Ernest Shackleton**. Amazingly enough, thousands of would-be volunteers and explorers lined up to be interviewed to be a part of his amazing and arduous adventure. We think we have it hard recruiting teams! ☺

- On August 3, 1913, a Canadian expedition sailed out on the *Karluk* to explore the Arctic between the North Pole and the northern most shores of Canada.

- On Dec 5th, 1914, the *Endurance* under the command of Ernest Shackleton sailed from South Georgia Island in the Southern Ocean. Their goal was the first overland crossing of Antarctica.

Both ships found themselves trapped in the ice pack and struggling for survival. The crew of the *Karluk* found themselves transformed into a group of self-interested, discouraged, lying, cheating individuals, eventually losing eleven to the Arctic challenges. Ernest Shackleton's *Endurance* crew proved to be just the opposite – teamwork, self-sacrifice, and even some good humour and attitudes were the norm in their team.

More amazingly, 634 days later, Sir Ernest Shackleton brought them all home. His inspiring leadership by example is one I have sought to emulate in my efforts.

I grew up with this story. *Trapped in the ice, ship crushed, living on the ice floes on the frozen Weddell Sea, challenging the raging Southern Ocean twice in an open longboat... being marooned on Elephant Island. The hazardous obstacles and adventure of sailing the* **James Caird** *for help, climbing mountains; and their eventual rescue on August 30th, 1916.* **Bringing them all back alive!**

Perhaps this was the source of my own drive to go to sea and eventually my 1988 perilous trip across the South Pacific from Hawaii to Japan; where the four of us encountered a 'baby' typhoon and almost lost our ship (SV John Pike).

Until I was about 11, I thought this story was about my uncle Ernest. My mom was a Shackleton (from Olds, Alberta) and her dad (my grandfather Fred immigrated to Canada from Britain via the US) was a cousin to Sir Ernest. My uncle Ernest (mom's older brother was named after him) was a teacher and school principal who taught me some lessons in life and leadership, as did his famous cousin and namesake.

Sir Ernest was no stranger to adventure. In 1909 he came within 97 nautical miles of the South Pole before he made the difficult decision to turn back. In that case, he chose the lives of his men over the fame of potential victory in reaching his goal. This was a part of who he was as a leader. He was committed to his team and wanted them to win. It was not about him. It was about the team accomplishment!

His sagas in the frozen Antarctic are one of legend. I will not attempt to cover it here. There are numerous books on his epic adventures.

As 21st Century leaders, we face constant challenges; challenges that are outside our control, such as natural disasters, climate, economic upheavals; challenges within our teams for survival and existence as a team; and challenges within ourselves for motivation, vision, and continued sense of purpose.

Let Sir Ernest Shackleton and his sagas be a lesson and guide in your leadership journey. (They just found Endurance below the ice)

I've had this framed advertisement (*torn from an old Saturday Evening Post*) on a wall in my office for nearly 27 years. It still provides idea-rich inspiration as I strive to enhance what I bring to the world.

Thanks for reading 'Legacy of Leadership'
Idea-rich strategies for *'serious'* leaders

Each time I prepare to step on the stage; each time I sit down to write, or in this case to re-write, I am challenged to ensure I deliver something that will be of **use-it-now value** to my reader.

- I ask myself, *"If I was reading this, what would I be looking for?"*
- As well as *"Why is this relevant to me, today?"*

These two questions help to keep me focused and help me to remain clear on my objectives. They help to remind me to dig into my experiences, stories, examples, and research to provide solid information that will be of benefit and help my readers, when they apply it, succeed. That can be an exciting challenge!

I trust I have done that for you in this updated primer. **'Legacy of Leadership'** is my attempt to capture some of the lessons learned *first-hand* serving on various teams and in leadership roles and to share them with you. We need more leaders, now, more than ever. The world is crying out for compassionate, courageous leaders. I hope you will step up and step into your role as a more effective and influential leader.

Bob in Mumbai, India

I'd love to hear from you and read your success stories. If you would be so kind, please drop me a quick email at: **bob@ideaman.net**

Bob 'Idea Man' Hooey
2011 Spirit of CAPS recipient
www.ideaman.net
www.HaveMouthWillTravel.com

Dedications

"Leadership is the heart and soul of exceptional team performance. The wise leader directs and unleashes the power and potential of those whom they would lead!"
Bob 'Idea Man' Hooey

- This print version, originally published as an e-publication, is dedicated to my many clients and fellow leaders who have taught me some *valuable* lessons in applied leadership.
- To my readers, audiences, and fellow leaders across the world who continue to share their ideas and experiences enhancing my own leadership journey. **To the men and women** who taught me by example by walking their talk as leaders.
- To my fellow Toastmasters, CAPS, NSA, and GSF leaders – friends like Neil Wilkinson, Chris Ford, John Noonan, Peter Kossowan, Greg Gazin, Terry Paulson, Patricia Katz, Dave Gordon, Lindsay Adams, Ravi Tangri, David Gouthro, Nabil Doss, Laura Stack, Ron Culbertson, Ruby Newell-Legner, and a host of others too numerous to name, who have encouraged my growth in leadership and service. The lessons were sometimes challenging, but the results were so worth it. To each of you, and many not named here, I owe a debt of gratitude.
- Dedicated as always, to my late parents who loved and encouraged me; to my sister Patti-Robin and her husband Jerry who always had time for me; and to my amazing wife Irene who patiently edited and proofed my writing.

I would like to take time to include specific dedications to outstanding individuals from the Alberta region whose leadership impacted mine for the better and whose friendship and leadership example I cherish.

I have chosen these three people to represent the many outstanding men and women who have helped me in my own leaders' journey.

The Honourable Lois Hole who passed away on January 6, 2005. She served with distinction as Alberta's Lieutenant Governor and made us all proud.

I've spoken at several events where this delightful woman spoke or was in attendance. Our first encounter was when I was the opening keynote for the Alberta Reeves, Mayors, and Councillors. I watched in amazement as she *hugged* her way in and out of the room. I was amazed at her *genuine* affection and love for the people she hugged. She spoke from her heart and captivated the audience, me included.

I had the distinct privilege of being **her official representative**, shortly after the death of her husband Ted, when she was unable to speak due to a reaction to the chemotherapy, she was taking to combat cancer. I was able to bring *official* greetings from her as the Queen's representative. I collected hugs and signatures on a get-well card, which I later delivered the hugs in person when she was back at work.

I still remember visiting her Edmonton office in the Alberta Legislature, sharing a tea and having her give me another warm hug as I left. I remember, too, a time in Staples when she saw me and came over to say hello and gave me a hug while I stood in line. She was a woman of *vision and leadership* who served Albertans with distinction. I am only one of thousands who very much miss her.

"I have faith in a better future, because I have faith that most human beings want to do the right thing. If we can put aside differences of ideology, if we can learn to love one another, then one day we will enjoy a world where no one need live in fear, where no one need go hungry, where everyone can enjoy a good education, the fellowship of friendly neighbors, and the security of a world at peace with itself at long last."
    **The Honorable Dr. Lois E. Hole, *C.M., A.O.E. (1933-2005)*
    Lieutenant Governor of Alberta**

Bill Comrie, O.C., founder of The Brick Warehouse Corporation, Canada's 2004 Entrepreneur of the Year

Bill's inspirational-leadership built Canada's largest volume furniture, appliance, bedding, and electronic chain – The Brick.

I had the *distinct privilege* of working alongside and assisting Bill for a over 5-years on a variety of projects including events where he was being honoured for his leadership and success in business. I may be the *'Idea Man',* but Bill is truly an *'Idea Machine'.* His creative mind and willingness to act are legendary. His vision in starting with $8000 and building a business that employed over 6000 people across Canada is legendary. He, however, is quick to share the credit with those he led.

"I want to make it clear that the inspiring growth and long-term success of The Brick was <u>never</u> 'just' about Bill Comrie. It was about the support and love of my family, a network of friends, and the <u>outstanding</u> efforts of 6000 of people on The Brick, Home Show, and United teams across Canada and the world."
Bill Comrie, Order of Canada

The **Legacy of Leadership** domain was originally earmarked for a book to be written about Bill's life and inspiring business leadership. However, upon his retirement and sale of a substantial part of his holdings (in which he personally gave close to $45 million to his employees); he decided, since he was now retired, to not go ahead with that publication.

I am indebted to Bill for his openness, kind friendship, focused encouragement, and dynamic example of true leadership. I have learned and continue to learn, first-hand from a true leadership champion and master. **"Thanks again, Bill!"**

Kim Yost, former President & CEO The Brick and retired CEO Art Van Furniture, Author Maximum Pumptitude

Kim Yost was personally recruited and mentored by Bill Comrie and dynamically led Team Brick to their next levels of success.

Kim was recruited to head up the **Art Van Furniture** chain in Michigan. Kim and his team have worked wonders, despite a sagging economy, in a challenged economic state. He has since retired.

Kim Yost is an energetic man, supportive friend, and dynamic leader, who *still* challenges me to think, to act, and to continue to grow. From our first meeting, he challenged me and has supported me in meeting and surpassing those challenges. I love him for it! He has been my cheerleader and champion for the past decade, plus. *I am so blessed!*

Kim is a dynamic, *engaging* leader, with a legendary retail track record, who sets and maintains a rapid pace of growth and strategic action. He is quick in his thoughts and grasp of challenges and even quicker in dealing with them. He inspires and leads by example and is constantly pushing past the comfort zone into the winner's zone. I have had the opportunity to work with Kim and his teams with both companies. I enjoy his continued influence and input in my own role as a leader. He is quick to challenge his team to push further and easily shares the victories in his encouraging manner. He invests himself in helping to equip his teams to grow and to win!

"Kim, thanks for continuing to challenge and teach me. You provide an amazing role model in applied leadership. I am privileged to call you friend."

Bring Bob 'Idea Man' Hooey in to work with you and your leadership team.

Perhaps your organization would like to bring Bob in to train, coach, and share a few leadership success ideas with your team.

Call him today: 1-780-736-0009 or email him at: bhooey@mcsnet.ca

Visit: **www.ideaman.net/Programs.html** for more information on his innovative leadership development programs. He can help you make a positive difference with your leadership.

Credits, copyrights, and disclaimers

Legacy of Leadership: *Idea-rich strategies for 'serious' leaders. Strive for significance – Lead with purpose!* *Expanded 6ᵗʰ edition*

By Bob 'Idea Man' Hooey, *Accredited Speaker, CKD-Emeritus*

Printed in the United States and Canada 10 9 8 7 6 5 4 3 2 1
First printing: 2006 **Updated: 2013, 2016, 2019, 2022, 2024**
Photos of Bob: **Dov Friedmann**, www.photographybyDov.com
Frédéric Bélot, www.fredericbelot.fr/fr
Bonnie-Jean McAllister, www.elantraphotography.com
Cover design: **Kat Doell**, https://www.instagram.com/kayhoganarts/
Editing: **Irene Gaudet**, www.VitrakCreative.com

Published by Success Publications - Canada
6ᵗʰ **Edition ISBN:** 978-1-998014-26-2 IS
© **Copyright 2006-2024** Bob 'Idea Man' Hooey – Ideas At Work!

SuccessPublications.ca
info@successpublications.ca
bhooey@mcsnet.ca
www.SuccessPublications.ca
Bob 'Idea Man' Hooey
Box 10, Egremont, AB T0A0Z0

We have not attempted to cite *all the authorities and sources* consulted in the preparation of this book. To do so would require much more space than is available. The list would include departments of various governments, libraries, industrial institutions, articles, clipping, notes, periodicals, and many individuals. Inspiration was drawn from many sources in the creation of **'Legacy of Leadership'**.

Disclaimer

About the author

Bob 'Idea Man' Hooey is a charismatic, confident leader, corporate trainer, inspiring facilitator, Emcee, prolific author, and motivational keynote speaker on leadership, creativity, sales success, business innovation, and enhancing team performance.

Using personal stories drawn from rich experience, he challenges his audiences to engage his **Ideas At Work! – To act on what they hear,** with clear, innovative building-blocks and field-proven success techniques to increase their effectiveness. Bob challenges them to hone specific 'success skills' critical to their personal and professional advancement.

Bob outlines real-life, results-based, innovative ideas personally drawn from 29 plus years of idea-rich leadership experience in retail, sales, construction, small business, entrepreneurship, manufacturing, association, consulting, community service, and commercial management.

Bob's conversational, often humorous, professional, and sometimes-provocative style continues to inspire and challenge his audiences across North America. Bob's motivational, innovative, challenging, and practical **Ideas At Work!** have been successfully applied by thousands of leaders and professionals across the globe.

Bob is a frequent contributor to North American consumer, corporate, association, trade, and on-line publications on leadership, sales success, employee motivation and training; as well as creativity and innovative problem solving, priority and time management, and effective customer service. He is the inspirational author of 30 plus publications including print, e-books, and a Pocket Wisdom series.

Retired, award winning kitchen designer, Bob Hooey, CKD-Emeritus was one of only 75 Canadian designers to earn this prestigious certification by the National Kitchen and Bath Association.

In December 2000, Bob was given a special CAPS National Presidential award **"…for his energetic contribution to the advancement of CAPS and his living example of the power of one"** in addition to being elected to the CAPS National Board.

Bob co-founded the CAPS BC Chapter, later serving as President. He was 2012 President of the CAPS Edmonton Chapter. He served on the National Board and the CAPS Foundation. He is an active leader in the National Speakers Association, the Canadian Association of Professional Speakers, as well as the Global Speakers Federation. In 2019 he helped found PSA-Spain and the VSAI in 2020.

In 1998, Toastmasters International recognized Bob **"…for his professionalism and outstanding achievements in public speaking"**. That August in Palm Desert, California Bob became the 48th speaker in the world to be awarded this prestigious professional level honor as an **Accredited Speaker**. He has been inducted into their Hall of Fame on numerous occasions for his leadership contributions.

Bob has been honoured by the United Nations Association of BC (1993) and received the **CANADA 125 award** (1992) for his ongoing contributions to the community. In 1998, Bob joined 3 other men to sail a 65-foot gaff rigged schooner from Honolulu, Hawaii to Kobe, Japan, barely surviving a *'baby'* typhoon enroute. **In November 2011, Bob was awarded the Spirit of CAPS** at their annual convention, becoming only the 11th speaker to earn this prestigious CAPS National award. Visit: **www.ideaman.net/SoC.htm**

Bob loves to travel, and his speaking and writing have allowed him to visit 71 countries on 6 continents so far (2024). Perhaps your organization would like to bring Bob in to share a few ideas with your leaders and teams, now on zoom. **www.HaveMouthWillTravel.com** for more information.

Bob's B.E.S.T. publications

Bob is a *prolific* author who has been capturing and sharing his wisdom and experience in print and electronic formats for the past fifteen plus years.

In addition to the following publications, several of them best sellers, he has written for consumer, corporate, professional associations, trade, and on-line publications.

He has been engaged to write and assist on publications by other best-selling writers and successful companies. His publications are listed to give you an idea of the scope and topics he writes about.
Bob's **B**usiness **E**nhancement **S**uccess **T**ools.

Leadership, business, and career development series

- **Running TOO Fast** (8th edition 2022)
- **Legacy of Leadership** (expanded 6th edition 2024)
- **Make ME Feel Special!** (6th edition 2022)
- **Why Didn't I 'THINK' of That?** (6th edition 2022)
- **Speaking for Success!** (expanded 10th edition 2023)
- **THINK Beyond the First Sale** (3rd edition 2022)
- **Prepare Yourself to Win!** (3rd edition 2017)
- **The early years… 1998-2009 – A Tip of the Hat collection**
- **The saga continues… 2010-2019 – A Tip of the Hat collection)**
- **Sales Success Secrets -2 volume set** (2021)

Bob's Mini-book success series

- **The Courage to Lead!** (4th edition 2017)
- **Creative Conflict** (3rd edition 2017)
- **Get to YES!** (expanded 5th edition 2023)

- **THINK Before You Ink!** (3rd edition 2017)
- **Running to Win!** (2nd edition 2017)
- **Generate More Sales** (expanded 5th edition 2023)
- **Sales Success -even in tough times** (5th edition 2023)
- **Unleash your Business Potential** (3rd edition 2017)
- **Maximize Meetings** (2019)
- **Learn to Listen** (2nd edition 2017)
- **Creativity Counts!** (updated 2016)
- **Create Your Future!** (3rd edition 2017)

Bob's Pocket Wisdom series

- **Pocket Wisdom for Speakers** (updated 2019)
- **Pocket Wisdom for Leaders – Power of One!** (updated 2019)
- Additional PW eBooks coming in 2024

Kindle Shorts (2017-2020) series - more to come in 2024

- **SPEAK!**
- **LEAD!**
- **SERVE!**
- **CREATE!**
- **CONFLICT!**
- **TIME!**

Co-authored books created by Bob

- **Quantum Success** – 3 volume series (2006)
- **In The Company of Leaders** (95th anniversary Edition 2019) We are working on a 100th anniversary edition for early 2024
- **Foundational Success** (2nd Edition 2013)

Visit: www.SuccessPublications.ca for more information on Bob's publications and other success resources.

What people say about Bob 'Idea Man' Hooey

As I travel across North America and around the globe, sharing my **Ideas At Work!**, I am fortunate to get feedback and comments from my audiences and colleagues. These comments come from people who have been touched, challenged, or simply enjoyed themselves in one of my sessions. **I'd love to come and share some ideas with your leaders and your organization.**

"As a past president of both the National Speakers Association and the Global Speakers Federation, I have had the opportunity of serving with and being served by Bob Hooey. His passion for the mission, his respect for the gifts of others on the team, and his confident humility to make a difference together was evident in all he did. His book, **Legacy of Leadership,** *provides a comprehensive and divergent window into inspiring leadership.* The quotes, tips, examples, and insights make this **a must read for any leader who doesn't want to settle for being anything less than the best they can be.** *"* Terry Paulson, PhD, CSP

"I have had the pleasure of knowing Bob for over 20 years through the Canadian Association of Professional Speakers. When I first met Bob, I became aware of the leadership he had provided to the local chapter here in Vancouver. **But that was only the tip of a leadership iceberg. Bob has continuously stepped up to provide leadership to our national organization** *in many capacities that have served our members at our annual conventions, chapter meetings, and through a recently set up charitable foundation. Not stopping there, he has also jumped in to provide direction and support to our sister organization in the US, the* **National Speakers Association, where he has provided guidance to new chapter leaders there, too.**

While I was President of CAPS (the Canadian Association of Professional Speakers), Bob's support from the trenches was always evident. Evidence of his multiple contributions was recognized by Bob receiving the **Spirit of CAPS award** *for longstanding contribution and service to our organization.*

Bob is a great role model for anyone wishing to take a leadership role, whether leading from the front or supporting from a bit further back!"
David Gouthro, CSP, Past CAPS National President

"I have known Bob Hooey for a number of years. During the entire period, Bob has proven himself again and again to be the consummate professional and a sterling leadership example. Since 1988, I have spoken, trained, and written about the elusive art of leadership in practice. **I have watched Bob as he has quietly exemplified what he calls the "Legacy of Leadership".** His book by the same name **is a primer for any and all who wish to make a difference and who are willing to work to leave a legacy." Phillip Van Hooser, CSP**, Past President, NSA, Author of 'Leaders Ought to Know: 11 Ground Rules for Common Sense Leadership'

"In his capacity as Chair of the Convention Committee of the philanthropic Foundation of the Canadian Association of Professional Speakers, Bob Hooey has exemplified the essence of leadership. He embraced his role with a pro-active mindset, an enthusiasm and energy that were contagious, and professional skill sets that spanned every aspect of his mandate. **Bob epitomizes the qualities of a leader: courage, commitment, and character. His leadership was one of the critical success factors in helping the CAPS Foundation not only achieve, but surpass, its fundraising objectives." Michael Hughes,** Chairman CAPS Foundation

"Bob 'Idea Man' Hooey is an exceptional speaker and facilitator who helps businesses and organizations grow profit and create effective teams. This leadership and sales expert has written 2 dozen books, travels the globe speaking to managers, corporations, and non-profits, increasing morale as well as profits. **Bob is a leader within the speaking industry and is beloved by his peers for his mentorship, warmth, and high skill.** I highly recommend Bob as a speaker. He'll be the one your employees and conference attendees talk about." **Shawne Duperon,** CEO, ShawneTV (3-time Emmy award winner)

"We greatly appreciate **the energy and effort you put into researching and adapting your keynote to make it more meaningful to our member councils.** *Early feedback from our delegates indicates that this year's convention was one of our most successful events yet, and we thank you for your contribution to this success."* **Larry Goodhope**, Executive Director Alberta Association of Municipal Districts and Counties

"Not only Bob is a trustful and highly professional expert, not only he is a fabulous and engaging speaker, Bob is also one of the nicest men I have ever met. He combines the wisdom of the experience with an astounding vigor and charisma. I highly recommend him. **Elizabeth Grimaud**, *AFCP (French Speakers Association)*

"Bob Hooey is a fabulous example of a confident, committed, and courageous leader. He doesn't just talk about effective leadership; he demonstrates it in all his endeavors. I met Bob through the National Speakers Association where we served together on the Chapter Leadership Committee. I found very quickly that we shared similar values and a commitment to assist others in reaching their leadership potential. *Bob's generosity and encouragement to those he served has become a model for the program.* In his fantastic book, *Legacy of Leadership*, Bob has created an outstanding overview of what it takes to be a leader in changing times. *This book is inspirational, insightful, and most importantly practical.* Read this book and you get to experience the coaching of a leader that has created a legacy".* **Steven Iwersen**, *Speaker & Author, Founder of Aurora Pointe - A Leadership Development Company*

"I've known Bob for several years and follow his activities in business with interest. I originally met Bob when he spoke for a Rotary Leadership Institute and got to know him better when he came to Vladivostok, Russia to speak to our leadership. **When you spoke, I thought you were one of us because you talked about our challenges just like yours.** You could understand the others, which makes you a great speaker!" **Andrey Konyushok**, Rotary International District 2225 Governor 2012-2013, far eastern Russia

"I watched Bob Hooey deliver a speech in Cape Town, SA when he was feeling far less than 100%. The audience never knew. That's what a pro does. Shows up and delivers!" **Shep Hyken**, CSP, CPAE, Past President NSA, professional speaker and customer service expert

*"Great seeing you in Cancun and congratulations on a job well done. **The seminar was a great success! Your humorous and conversational style was a tremendous asset.*** It is my sincere hope that we can be associated again at future seminars."* **Donald MacPherson**, Attorney At Law, Phoenix, Arizona

*"I am pleased to recommend Bob 'Idea Man' Hooey to any organization looking for a charismatic, confident speaker and seminar leader. I have seen Bob in action on several occasions, and he is ALWAYS on! Bob has the ability to grab his audience's attention and keep it. Quite simply, **if Bob is involved - your program or seminar is guaranteed to succeed.***" **Maurice Laving**, Coordinator Training and Development, London Drugs

"Dear Mr. Hooey: **Thank you for elevating my Sales Team's knowledge during your sales management seminar in Tehran, Iran.** I look forward to meeting you in person during your future seminars. Warm regards." **Mendi Ghaemi**, Managing Director, Bidar Group

"As the International President of the *Global Speakers Federation* I have seen many speakers present in the last 12 months around the world. *Bob 'Idea Man' Hooey is one of the most outstanding speakers I have seen and worked with.* He truly walks his talk and is a fountain of ideas and innovation in his presentation on stage and in his dealings off stage. I recommend Bob to anyone who is seeking a dynamic speaker who will bring something interesting, thought provoking and fun every time he gets up to speak." **Lindsay Adams, *CSP***

"I had the pleasure of hearing and watching Bob Hooey deliver a keynote speech several years ago when he gave a presentation at a Toastmasters International Convention. **Bob impressed me greatly with his professionalism, energy, and ability to connect with his audience while giving them value.** I heartily recommend this talented speaker and 'Idea Man' to all who want to move to the next level." **Dr. Dilip Abayasekara, DTM, Accredited Speaker,** Past Toastmasters International President

*"Thank you, Bob; it is **always a pleasure to see a true professional at work.** You have made the name "Speaker" stand out as a truism - someone who encourages people to examine their lives and make adjustments. The personal stories you shared with your audience made such a great impression on everyone. **The comments indicated you hit people right where it is important - in their hearts.** Each of those in your audience took away a new feeling of personal success and encouragement."* **Sherry Knight,** Dimension Eleven Human Resources and Communications

---

Connect with Bob 'Idea Man' Hooey:

- **Facebook:** www.facebook.com/bob.hooey
- **LinkedIn:** www.linkedin.com/in/canadianideamanbobhooey
- **YouTube:** www.youtube.com/ideamanbob
- **Smashwords:** www.smashwords.com/profile/view/Hooey
- **Email:** bob@ideaman.net or bhooey@mcsnet.ca
- Creative Office: 780-736-0009
- **Snail mail:** PO Box 10, Egremont, AB T0A0Z0
- **Amazon:** www.amazon.com/Bob-Idea-Man-Hooey/e/B00FACOHNY

Engage Bob for your leaders and their teams

"I have been so excited working with Bob Hooey, as he has given inspiration and motivation to our leadership team members. Both at the Brick Warehouse – Alberta and here at Art Van Furniture – Michigan; with his years of experience in working with business executives and his humorous and delightful packaging of his material, he makes learning with Bob a real joy. But most importantly, anyone who comes in contact with his material is the better for it."
Kim Yost, retired CEO Art Van Furniture, former CEO The Brick

Motivate your teams, your employees, and your leaders to *productively* grow and *profitably* succeed!

- Protect your conference investment - leverage your training dollars.
- Enhance your professional career and sell more products and services.
- Equip and motivate your leaders and their teams to grow and succeed, 'even' in tough times!
- Leverage your leadership to leave a significant legacy!

Call today to engage inspirational leadership keynote speaker, sales leaders' success coach, and employee development trainer, **Bob 'Idea Man' Hooey** and his innovative, audience based, results-focused, **Ideas At Work!** for your next company, convention, leadership, staff, sales, training, or association event. You'll be glad you did!

Call 1-780-736-0009 to connect with Bob 'Idea Man' Hooey today!

www.ingramcontent.com/pod-product-compliance
Lightning Source LLC
Chambersburg PA
CBHW071702210326
41597CB00017B/2302